An Introduction to Fictional Worlds Theory

LITERARY AND CULTURAL THEORY

General Editor: Wojciech H. Kalaga

VOLUME 43

PETER LANG
EDITION

Bohumil Fořt

An Introduction
to Fictional
Worlds Theory

PETER LANG
EDITION

Bibliographic Information published by the Deutsche Nationalbibliothek
The Deutsche Nationalbibliothek lists this publication in the Deutsche Nationalbibliografie; detailed bibliographic data is available in the internet at http://dnb.d-nb.de.

Library of Congress Cataloging-in-Publication Data
Names: Fořt, Bohumil.
Title: An introduction to fictional worlds theory / Bohumil Fořt.
Description: Frankfurt am Main ; New York : Peter Lang, 2016. | Series: Literary and cultural theory ; Volume 43
Identifiers: LCCN 2015038827 | ISBN 9783631670767
Subjects: LCSH: Fiction–Technique. | Literature–Aesthetics. | Intertextuality. | Narration (Rhetoric) | Storytelling.
Classification: LCC PN3355 .F58 2016 | DDC 808.3–dc23 LC record available at http://lccn.loc.gov/2015038827

This book has been published with financial support by the Faculty of Arts of Masaryk University in Brno, Czech Republic.

ISSN 1434-0313
ISBN 978-3-631-67076-7 (Print)
E-ISBN 978-3-653-06323-3 (E-Book)
DOI 10.3726/978-3-653-06323-3

© Peter Lang GmbH
Internationaler Verlag der Wissenschaften
Frankfurt am Main 2016
All rights reserved.
Peter Lang Edition is an Imprint of Peter Lang GmbH.

Peter Lang – Frankfurt am Main · Bern · Bruxelles · New York · Oxford · Warszawa · Wien

This publication has been peer reviewed.

www.peterlang.com

To my family

Contents

Foreword

Why fictional worlds? There is no one simple answer – indeed, an exhaustive answer would encompass a whole set of partial answers demarcated by intuition on the one hand and by a methodological need on the other. The aforementioned intuition is connected with the fascinating idea that when reading fictional texts we actually *enter* (fictional) worlds, as is well known to everybody who embarks on the stunning adventure of reading fiction. Nevertheless, this idea of entering literary worlds is by no means new and is not merely a development of the *fictional worlds theory*; however, this theory articulates this idea freshly and cultivates it in a systematic way. It does so by means of the sources of methodological inspiration on which the fictional worlds theory is founded: the theory is firmly bound to *logic* via *possible worlds* and to *linguistics* via the methods of *style analyses*.

When the first signs of the newly developing theory appeared in literary theoretical inquiry in the 1970s and, in particular, in the 1980s, it very quickly became clear that possible worlds of logic embodied the most important source of inspiration for fictional worlds – to the extent that some scholars referred to *fictional worlds* as to *possible worlds of literature*. Today, it is obvious that fictional worlds and possible worlds cannot be considered identical and that the inspiration of the fictional by the possible worlds is rather of a metaphorical type: possible worlds are universes of logical statements and are subordinated to strict logical rules, whereas fictional worlds are based in fictional texts and are "brought to life" by the mental activity of the reader during the act of reading. Nevertheless, it has to be argued that the fictional worlds theory actually profits from possible worlds of logical discourse by borrowing several concepts and strategies of their logical inquiry; among these, the most important are connected with the issue of reference, trans-world-identity, and the relation of accessibility as the following chapters of this book will demonstrate. Therefore, the first chapter of my book is devoted to key concepts of logical possible worlds, which seem to be crucial for the development and the final form of fictional worlds. In this chapter, I attempt not only to examine the crucial concepts of logical possible worlds and their qualities, but also, to show the inspiration of possible worlds for modern semiotics and linguistics.

The entire second chapter of the book deals with fictional worlds. I must admit that the ideas involved in this part are mainly centred around Lubomír Doležel's contributions to fictional worlds theory. His suggestions serve as a basis for analysing various aspects and levels of fictional worlds; however, I also carefully examine, analyse, and value the contributions of other fictional worlds theoreticians; such as, Umberto Eco, Thomas Pavel, Ruth Ronen, and Marie-Laure Ryan. The main reason for placing Doležel's suggestions at the centre of my attention in this chapter is that he articulates the difference between the *extensional* and *intensional structure* of fictional worlds: whereas, the former refers to subjects, objects and their actions within fictional worlds, the latter denotes the ways in which fictional worlds are anchored in languages. Fictional worlds are encoded in languages and decoded from them; therefore, the style analysis of fictional texts offers an important source for their analysis. Indeed, the so called intensional functions, defined as functions operating from literary texts to fictional worlds and serving to structure these worlds, are a telling example of the application of linguistic concepts to fictional worlds. A detailed analysis of the intensional functions and their qualities and connections to other literary theoretical concepts creates the core of this chapter.

The third chapter of the book is devoted to the notion of intertextuality, which is examined using the tools offered by the fictional worlds theory. Here, I examine the notion of *transduction*, as it has been introduced to the realm of fictional worlds inquiry, and its role in intertextual investigation. The notion of transduction actually enables us to compare fictional texts at the level of fictional worlds, which are based on these fictional texts. As a result, the comparison of literary artworks based on the comparison of the fictional worlds they produce encompasses various levels of possible connections of these artworks.

Finally, the fourth chapter examines the connections between fictional worlds and the Prague (Structuralist) School. Since I consider Lubomír Doležel's contribution to the fictional worlds theory crucial, in this chapter, I put his theoretical background under close examination and show how the achievements of the Prague School's structuralist approach to literary artworks shaped the theory of fictional worlds.

The fictional worlds theory has undertaken a rather rapid development in the last four decades and has inspired many scholars who do not primarily deal with fictional worlds to implement some of the ideas developed in the fictional worlds realm into their scholarly work. *An Introduction into Fictional Worlds Semantics*, I hope, represents a relatively concise and accessible path to the crucial ideas of the fictional worlds theory and also uncovers the wider context of the origin and development of the theory.

Obviously, this book, as any other book, could not have been finished without the support of many people and institutions. Here, I would like to thank all three universities that were somehow (and at the same time, crucially) involved in the writing of the book: The University of Toronto, The University of London and my home, Masaryk University in Brno, and especially their wonderful libraries, and, last but not least, the Institute of Czech Literature of The Czech Academy of Sciences for all its institutional support. I would also like to thank all the people who supported me during the writing process of this book – they know who they are; however, Brian Locke deserves special thanks for his tremendous help with the manuscript. Nevertheless, my warmest thanks go to Lubomír Doležel, my dear friend and mentor, without whom fictional worlds might not have been a part of my real world.

I. Possible worlds

1. The notion of possible worlds

The concept of possible worlds is originally connected with the name of Saul Kripke and has become one of the most useful concepts in the field of modern logical semantics. Alvin Plantinga, another prominent logician, straightforwardly asserts that a possible world is "a way things could have been" (PLANTINGA 1974: 44). On the one hand, this general description of the notion of possible worlds sufficiently explains the merit of the notion; on the other, it is general to the extent that it allows almost any approach in the humanities and sciences to adopt it and use it for their own purposes. For now, we can stick to the claim that fictional worlds are (possible) sets of *states of affairs*; this statement represents the most common and frequent understanding of the term.

The motivation of the development of possible worlds becomes clear when one focuses thoroughly on the most frequently employed description of possible worlds: "The idea is roughly this: we can all imagine that the world we live in could be somewhat different from what it in reality is, and we also seem to be able to talk meaningfully about what would happen if the world were different, as in the following sentence: 'If it had not rained this morning, we would have gone to the country.' We can thus say that there are several 'ways in which the world could have been'. Instead of this complex expression we will use the shorter expression 'possible world'" (ALLWOOD-ANDERSSON-DAHL 1977: 22).

Saul Kripke, in his *Naming and Necessity* (1980), used the notion of possible worlds as the basis for his own system of intensional logic: an intension of a statement is the statement's extension related to a possible world, i.e., a function that relates every possible world to an extension of all statements in this world. Kripke strives to develop a semantic system encompassing modal operators; such as, necessity and possibility. Possible worlds semantics thus becomes an adequate tool for fulfilling this aim. Most logicians seem to agree that possible world semantics helps them to avoid some of the difficulties involved in classical approaches to logic. One logician, Wolfgang Heydrich, comments on the motivation of introducing possible worlds to logic explicitly: "The basic intuition is about the nature of modality, and it consists in the leading idea that possibility amounts to a pre-fabricated space of *all* the consistent and complete ways the world is or might have been" (HEYDRICH 1989: 189).

But what is a possible world? What is its status? What exactly does David Lewis mean when he stipulates that, "Possible worlds are what they are and not

13

some other thing" (LEWIS 1973: 85)? We first need to explore some of the basic characteristics of the concept of possible worlds.

At the beginning of an investigation of possible worlds it should be emphasised that the notion itself was originally introduced by Gottfried Wilhelm Leibniz in his book, *Theodicea* (1710). Nevertheless, Leibniz uses this notion purely for the purposes of the building of his own metaphysical system.[1] Clearly, modern logic does not insist on the metaphysical background of fictional worlds any more. As Jaroslav Peregrin suggests, "One way is to view possible worlds as instruments of certain empirical features of a language (of modal statements and their semantic properties, in particular), where their acceptance is based on a belief that these worlds are useful tools in providing a simple and transparent solution to the problems that have led us to an abandonment of extensional semantics. Taking a different perspective, we can start to examine the essence of statements, meanings, worlds and truth and come to the conclusion that, besides our actual world, there are many non-actualized possible worlds, and that the meanings of statements are relative to the worlds in which they are true. This path can be assigned as 'speculative-metaphorical'" (PEREGRIN 1998: 93–94). According to this statement, it is possible to submit the notion of possible worlds to a metaphysical inquiry; however, the way in which the term is used in logical semantics refers more or less to the first way suggested above by Peregrin – as we will see later, this can be found especially in the approach of Richard Montague, who uses sets of logical possibilities to evaluate modal statements in natural language; these sets are, in fact, possible worlds of contemporary logic.

So far it has been said that the notion of possible worlds is especially bound to logical semantics and also that the term has been extensively researched and explored on this basis as a useful tool for intensional logic. Nevertheless, since it was first used by Saul Kripke this term has been taken on a life of its own and has become an object of mainly epistemological inquiry. An analysis of the term,

---

1 For the final shape of the notion of possible world which represents the highest stage of Leibniz's ontology, the relationship between parts and wholes are of particular importance and Leibniz strictly differentiates between *qualitative* and *quantitative* wholes. In his *Theodicea* he emphasises that God has actualised the best one of all possible worlds which has become real. The fact that the *best* of all worlds has been actualised does not imply that this world is the best one in all of its parts: regardless of the fact that some of its parts can be worse than parts of worlds which have not been actualised the actual world is the best one as a whole. Obviously, this world represents a qualitative whole – had it been a quantitative one its parts would include all the properties of the whole.

possible worlds, follows two main directions: it aims to assign the sets of qualities necessary for possible worlds and also to establish a typology of these worlds. Nevertheless, both directions are complementary and also commonly combined in analyses of possible worlds. When speaking about analysing possible worlds it should be emphasised that, although based in logical discourse, possible worlds are also often reimagined and re-narrated against other backgrounds. This development is firmly connected to the fact that possible worlds have become attractive for other areas of the humanities and sciences besides logic.

An important epistemological constraint appears in the realm of possible worlds and their logical basis. Possible worlds are "stipulated" by language and therefore, the epistemological status of the entities of which these worlds consist is a discursive one: possible worlds and their entities are simply subsets of the universe of discourse. If this is so, an important question needs to be raised: Can possible worlds really be considered states of affairs, as suggested above? Probably not. Pavel Materna voices a reason why possible worlds cannot be accepted as states of affairs and connects this view with Ludwig Wittgenstein: "*World* is here not a collection of things (together with their properties and relations): it would be fully unjustified and irrational to suppose that there could be more than one world in this sense. A better approximation is obtained if 'world' is interpreted in the spirit of Wittgenstein as denoting a collection of (possible, consistently thinkable) *facts*. [...] Thus we could say (very informally) that a *possible world is a collection of thinkable facts*; one of such collections is the real, '*actual*' world" (MATERNA 1998: 25). Another Czech logician, Pavel Tichý, argues similarly when criticising David Lewis' view that a possible world is equal to a totality of things: "David Lewis, who advocates this totality-of-things notion of possible world, has a reply to this. The things that populate alternative worlds, he says, are located in 'alternative spaces'. To say this, however, is to compound one absurdity with a worse one. Space is by definition all-embracing. It is bad enough to allow for *material bodies* that escape its reach. It defies reason to assume that space leaves room for other fully-blown *spaces* for those bodies to be located in. The question 'Where?' is tantamount to 'Whereabout in space?'. A planet which is not in space is nowhere; and a planet which is not anywhere is not at all" (TICHÝ 1988: 178). Like Materna, Tichý also finds support for his view regarding possible worlds in the work of Wittgenstein: "The objection to the idea of alternative worlds becomes forceless, however, if instead of saying with Lewis that a world is a totality of *things*, we say with Wittgenstein that it is a totality of (possible) *facts*" (178). Tichý's own contribution to possible worlds will be elaborated on further below.

As much as Materna's and Tichý's arguments illuminate the very notion of possible worlds in the sense that they should not be, strictly speaking, considered states of affairs, it is fair to say that the view of possible worlds as states of affairs can already be discovered in the work of the founder of the concept of possible worlds, Saul Kripke, who metaphorically describes the way in which possible worlds exist: "A possible world is not a distant country that we are coming across, or viewing through a telescope. Generally speaking, another possible world is too far away [...] A possible world is *given by the descriptive conditions we associate with it* [...] Possible worlds are *stipulated*, not *discovered* by powerful telescopes" (KRIPKE 1980: 44). Thus, possible worlds are inseparable from the language in which they exist – Charles Chihara uses Kripke's metaphor in order to describe Plantinga's contribution to possible worlds theory: "there is no such thing as looking into these worlds and finding some real person" (CHIHARA 1998: 59).

On the one hand, this terminological division can be considered too rigid, but on the other, an overly flexible terminological usage can lead to problems with the ontological status of possible worlds and this aspect is crucial for any theoretical inquiry and the use of the concept at all. This especially applies to rigid logical conceptions that use possible worlds for solving specific logical tasks. However, at this point it should be mentioned that not all scholars discount the notion of possible worlds as states of affairs.[2] As we will see later, this view is profitable for the after-life of possible worlds.

2. The qualities of possible worlds

So far we have considered several descriptions of possible worlds and it is obvious now that, in addition to strict definitions and rigid descriptions, we can encounter somewhat metaphorical or figurative formulations in connection with this notion. This attitude seems to be common to some of the scholars who deal with the notion for specific purposes – thus, instead of defining possible worlds rigidly they characterise them in terms of describing both their essential as well as accidental qualities. These descriptions can vary depending on different attitudes to possible worlds and their analyses. Nevertheless, the majority of the possible worlds of different scholars overlap in terms of their basic features, which can be considered as essential for the rest of this study.

---

2   For example the above mentioned Prior and Fine at the very beginning of their approach to the question that possible worlds are possible states of affairs, nevertheless they do not represent "real individuals" (PRIOR & FINE 1977: 53).

1. Logical consistency. Possible worlds are logically consistent (i.e., non-contradictory): a possible world cannot encompass both a statement A and its contradiction ¬A at the same time. This rule is essential for possible worlds in order for them to maintain their truth-values. If a statement and its negation were both true in one fictional world then all the statements in this world entailed from these statements would be true: from a contradiction anything can be entailed.

2. Logical completeness. Logical semantics considers possible worlds to be complete entities. This, again, is crucial in terms of truth-values: any statement within a possible world, which represents a logical universe, should be able to have a truth-value.

3. Validity of logical implication. To all possible worlds the following logical operation applies: if there exists a set of true statements (in any logical universe) from which another true statement can be implied, this statement is true in the same logical universe.

3. Identification in possible worlds

In this section we consider another topic which is central to the concept of possible worlds – that of identity. It has been said that possible worlds are (sometimes) considered states of affairs. When approaching possible worlds and their entities from an ontological point of view, one necessarily encounters a question: Is the same entity identical in all possible worlds? Obviously, this question can be answered only in the following way: "Apparently not all objects existing in one world also exist in all others" (KUTSCHERA 1975: 187). If this statement were false there would be just one self-identical world. The only way to examine the identity of entities in possible worlds is to find them in the worlds in which they exist and examine them.[3] Franz von Kutschera points out three different attitudes to this task:

a) Particular things are independent of their qualities and "then there may be the same objects in different worlds" (187). It would seem that this solution does not offer us much in the way of epistemological profit.

b) Particular things can be identified only with regard to their qualities: "In fact we should say that two objects that have different *essential* properties

---

3 For example Willard van Orman Quine views the issue of trans-world similarity as a direct result of investigation into the relationships between individuals in different fictional worlds – see esp. Quine 1981, pg. 128.

cannot be identical" (188). This solution leads us to the notion of a *trans-world-identity*.

c)   Particular things exist only in one particular world. Objects of two different sets of states of affairs cannot be identical: they can be only similar. This solution refers to what in the modern logical context is known as *counterpart theory*.

3.1 Trans-world-identity (TWI)

In the logical semantics of possible worlds, the second attitude listed above by Kutschera seems to be the most common one. The main question can then be formulated as follows: What are the essential properties of a particular thing that determine the thing in all possible worlds in which that thing exists? Nicolas Rescher offers us an answer to this question: "The theory of possible worlds and the theory of essentialism are intimately intertwined because possible worlds and essential properties stand in mutually reciprocal coordination. It is very much a matter of which end of the stick one is to pick up" (RESCHER 1975: 77). Let us recall that from the time of Aristotle, theoreticians have referred to two kinds of qualities: *essential* (*necessary*) qualities, which are necessary and essential for a thing to be the thing it really is, and *accidental* properties, which are not essential to the nature of the thing; the thing obtains them only possibly, accidentally. For the notion of trans-world-identity this division between kinds of properties is crucial. Necessary properties are properties "that an object has in all possible worlds" (LINSKY 1969: 698). Nevertheless, another question can be raised: Which are the qualities that allow us to refer to the same individual in two different possible worlds?

It seems that in order to answer the above question we have two paths from which to choose. Rescher describes two possible approaches to an analysis of possible worlds within the essentialist realm: "One can start by taking possible worlds as somehow given (never mind how!), and then introduce essentiality on this basis, defining an essential property of a thing as one that it has in every possible world. Or one can approach the issue the other way round. Starting with essentiality-imputations one can proceed to determine possible worlds on this basis. Abstractly speaking, either approach is possible" (RESCHER 1975: 77).

The first approach is logically very straightforward and elegant and makes us formulate the essential quality that an object keeps in all possible worlds – the criterion of identity. If we do not try to apply this criterion outside the realm of logically developed possible worlds, we avoid all paradoxes and problems connected with the empirical search for identity in the qualities of individuals. Logic simply proclaims the essential qualities of objects and thus founds the identity of the object.

The second approach referred to by Rescher is, for the purpose of possible worlds, rather inconvenient. The reason is that the possible worlds are commonly felt as given, and thus we do not have access to the way in which they are constructed.

3.1.1 Kripke's notion of transworld identity

Saul Kripke, when speaking about an object's qualities in possible worlds, prefers the second of the approaches mentioned by Nicolas Rescher above. Kripke admits that to offer a general criterion for the identity of objects is difficult; however, he tries to solve the issue of TWI in a specific logical way and thus reserves the term *designator* for names and descriptions. In addition, Kripke introduces the term *rigid designator*: "Let us call something a *rigid designator* if in every possible world it designates the same object" (KRIPKE 1980: 48). Further, according to Kripke, whereas proper names represent rigid designators, descriptions do not. Consequently, Kripke provides an example supporting his definition: "Those who have argued that to make sense of the notion of rigid designator, we must antecedently make sense of 'criteria of transworld identity' have precisely reversed the cart and the horse; it is *because* we can refer (rigidly) to Nixon, and stipulate that we are speaking of what might have happened to *him* (under certain circumstances), that 'transworld identifications' are unproblematic in such cases" (49).

In his further investigation, Kripke stays with his definition of possible worlds as strictly logically based entities and this approach informs his view of their objects which, according to his definition, differ from real entities: "What I do deny is that a particular is nothing but a 'bundle of qualities', whatever that may mean. If a quality is an abstract object, a bundle of qualities is an object of an even higher degree of abstraction, not a particular. Philosophers have come to the opposite view through a false dilemma: they have asked, are these objects *behind* the bundle of qualities, or is the object *nothing but* the bundle? Neither is the case; this table is wooden, brown, in the room, etc. It has all these properties and is not a thing without properties, behind them; but it should not therefore be identified with the set, or 'bundle', of its properties, nor with the subset of its essential properties. Do not ask: How can I identify this table in another possible world, except by its properties? I have the table in my hands, I can point to it, and when I ask whether *it* might have been in another room, I am talking, by definition, about *it*. I do not have to identify it after seeing it through a telescope.

If I am talking about it, I am talking about *it*, in the same way as when I say that our hands might have been painted green, I have stipulated that I am talking about greenness. Some properties of an object may be essential to it, in that it could not have failed to have them. But these properties are not used to identify the object in another possible world, for such an identification is not *needed*" (KRIPKE 1980: 52–53).[4]

At the very end of his reasoning Kripke explicitly adopts a position close to the so-called semantically atomised approach to possible worlds. This approach considers all the objects shared by different possible worlds to be the same, thanks to their logical origin: "We can refer to the object and ask what might have happened to *it*. So, we do not begin with worlds, and then ask about criteria of transworld identification; on the contrary, we begin with the objects, which we *have*, and can identify, in the actual world. We can then ask whether certain things might have been true of the objects" (KRIPKE 1980: 53).

3.1.2 Rescher's possible worlds and TWI

Rescher, in contrast to Kripke, who atomically proceeds from individuals to possible worlds focuses on the moment of construction of possible worlds.[5] He constructs possible worlds from their basic elements: possible individuals. "The population of a possible world will, of course, consist of possible individuals (in a sense which includes the actual): possible worlds simply *are* collections of possible individuals duly combined with one another. Our 'constructive' approach proceeds by way of moving first to possible individuals, and then, with these *prefabricated* individuals at our disposal, proceeding to stock the various possible worlds with this population" (RESCHER 1975, 78). When Rescher defines possible worlds "from below" he raises a question as to whether a possible world is determined by any set of individuals. This question naturally produces a response that possible worlds do not work in this way. In possible worlds, there exist individuals that can coexist in one possible world and individuals that cannot. This impossibility of the co-existence of some individuals in one possible world has a

---

4 All quotations contain emphais in the original, unless explicitly stated otherwise.
5 Generally speaking, Kripke's and Rescher's intensions are very similar, nevertheless, unlike Kripke, Rescher explicitly points out the process of the contruction of possible worlds from their individuals.

basis that is at the same time logical (it challenges the logical rules of possibility), nomical (individuals challenge natural laws), and metaphysical.[6]

The fact that Rescher proceeds from possible individuals towards fictional worlds brings him to another important issue: to the issue of the identity of possible individuals. Consequently, Rescher distinguishes between two kinds of identity: strict (S-Identity) and generic (G-Identity). The G-Identity is determined by an equivalence of the individuals that mutually correspond in all possible worlds; therefore, we can clearly see that G-Identity is in fact a TWI. In the case of a constructive approach to possible worlds (where possible worlds consist of pre-fabricated possible individuals), the notion of a TWI does not cause any problems: "*Trans*-world identity is resolved in terms of *pre*-world identity. Since possible worlds are stocked with *prefabricated* individuals, the issue of reidentification cannot prove problematic" (RESCHER 1975: 87). In other words, Rescher "builds" possible worlds from particular possible individuals and therefore needs not look for the qualities the individuals have in common in all possible worlds in which they exist. This form of rigid essentialism leads Rescher to the following statement: "In our approach, the very individuation of the individual provides the key to trans-world identification: its identity follows an individual as unfailing through different possible worlds as a person's shadow" (87–88).

At this point, it should be emphasised that Rescher's conception of identity fully fits his "from below" system: "Once we take ourselves to be dealing with an individual and hypothetically modifying *it*, then it remains self-identically on our hands throughout. The survival of identity through all (logico-metaphysically admissible) hypothetical alterations is a basic principle of our theory" (RESCHER 1985: 88). Thus, from Rescher's perspective, the same individual can be found in different possible worlds. From an epistemological point of view it is important to make sure that these individuals are first of all well demarcated and well defined. However, this can be done only within the realm of one particular possible world: "If a possible world is to be fully determinate and well-defined, one must not just be able to *describe* its contents taken in isolation, but also, by fully individuating its members, be able to relate them to those of the actual and of other possible worlds. Accordingly, the following two items must be included

---

6   As we can see, at this point Rescher places logical co-possibility in first place. However, his possible worlds are bound to the possible worlds of logics – due to their transcendence of nomical and metaphysical aspects of possible worlds: "A 'possible world' is one that not merely consists of possible individuals, but satisfies certain metaphysical considerations as to the 'compossibility' of individuals capable of copresence in one common world" (RESCHER 1975: 84).

in the adequate specification of a possible world: 1) the essentialistically complete descriptive specification (C.D.S.) of the various individuals that constitute the population of the world; 2) the specification of which individuals are to be surrogates for actual individuals—and just which actual individuals. In sum, if a possible world is to be well defined, then its membership must be specified by information sufficient actually to *individuate* its members: One must be in a position to determine the *fic* for every individual comprised in a possible world" (89–90).

Rescher disagrees with what he considers the dominant view of TWI among theorists and states that the whole notion of TWI cannot be sorted out by taking two possible worlds and comparing their individuals: "Unsolvability arises because the problem is about the identity of individuals in circumstances where information crucial to their identification has deliberately been suppressed" (RESCHER 1985: 91). This issue depends entirely on the idea that possible worlds are commonly considered already given entities, which is incongruent with Rescher's own constructivist conception that views possible worlds thus: "Possible worlds are never 'given' from on high, they are made up, manufactured as assumption-contexts where the issue of the nature of their ingredients must in principle be resolvable and may well actually have to be resolved if certain questions are to be answerable. The make-up of possible worlds must not be allowed to baffle us – we enjoy mastery over their descriptive detail precisely because they are products of our own devising" (91).

To describe the entities of worlds is a strategy that does not fully suffice to demarcate a possible world. This fact is directly connected with the issue of TWI: "That such incomplete information does not enable us to resolve the issue of trans-world identity is a matter of course. But once the crucial facts about actuality-relatedness are added to descriptive information, then the process of individuation is complete, and we are actually in a position to settle questions of trans-world identification in a relatively straightforward way" (90).

Let us repeat that Rescher's possible worlds are not sums of individuals. Proceeding from the developed principles of co-possibility for individuals, Rescher introduces the concept of *environment* and claims that "individuals are *not* (or *need* not be) wholly independent of their environing world. We cannot put an individual into any world-environment we please" (RESCHER 1985: 93–94). Mainly for logical reasons, some individuals simply cannot be accommodated within the same possible world. For the same reasons, there are individuals that must be situated in the some worlds together with other individuals. At this point, it is clear that Rescher is referring to Leibniz's *monads* with their *windows*;

Rescher explicitly states that they are not "windowless." However, the difference between monads and Rescher's possible worlds lies in the fact that Rescher's worlds are primarily mereological sums: "Possible worlds just *are* certain collections of possible individuals. The features of such worlds are what they are because they consist of certain individuals" (94). On the one hand, individuals in possible worlds are prefabricated, in that they exist prior to possible worlds and possible worlds are sums of these individuals; on the other, these sums are determined by their individuals: "Worlds impose no "emergent" features on their individuals, features which could not in principle be determined to hold of these individuals considered in separation, without reference to world environments" (94).

3.2 Counterpart theory

The counterpart theory is primarily connected with the name of David Lewis, who offers his own concept as an alternative to TWI.[7] The proposed counterpart theory actually stems from Lewis' indexical attitude towards actuality: "The counterpart relation is our substitute for identity between things in different worlds. Where some would say that you are in several worlds, in which you have somewhat different properties and somewhat different things happen to you, I prefer to say that you are in the actual world and no other, but you have counterparts in several other worlds. But they are not really you. For each of them is in his own world, and only you are here in the actual world. Indeed, we might say, speaking casually, that your counterparts are you in other worlds, that they and you are the same; but this sameness is no more a literal identity" (LEWIS 1968: 114). Furthermore, Lewis claims that he is able to avoid some of the problematic issues faced by various theories of (trans-world) identity by introducing the term *trans-world resemblance*: "What comes from trans-world resemblance is not trans-world identity but a substitute for trans-world identity: the counterpart relation. [...] In general: something has for *counterparts* at a given world those things existing there that resemble it closely enough in important respects of intrinsic quality and extrinsic relations, and that resemble it not less closely than do other things existing there" (LEWIS 1973: 39). At first sight, Lewis' theory seems to be unproblematic and even attractive in terms of its potential applications;

---

7   The reason for doing this is an attempt to avoid the complex issue of assessing the identity of individuals: "The unactualized possibles I do believe in confined each to his own world and united only by ties of resemblance to thein counterparts elsewhere do not pose any special problem of individuation" (LEWIS 1973: 87).

however, it is obvious that his approach in fact necessitates a step away from a rigid logical view of possible worlds. This conception of the relationship between possible worlds and the actual world (a point more thoroughly elaborated in the next chapter) reaches the point where his possible worlds are not accessible via a united language; therefore, the relation of a counterpart necessarily dissolves in the context of particular worlds. Furthermore, it is clear that there are many such relationships dependent on the contextual factors of the notion 'resemblance'.

Rescher summarises Lewis' theory and points to its aims: 1) to dismiss the notion of TWI and stipulate that no two individuals existing in two different possible worlds are not identical; 2) to replace the notion of TWI with the notion of the counterpart, which is based on the relationship of similarity. Nevertheless, Rescher also joins the group of critics of Lewis and indicates the problems connected with his notion of 'sufficient-similarity', which in Lewis' conception is firmly connected with *degrees* of similarity. Rescher raises the following question: What is the 'sufficient-similarity' that guarantees that the individuals we deal with are actually connected by the counterpart-relationship? Consequently, he comes to the conclusion: "Thus the conditions of counterparthood would be three: shared essence, close resemblance, and locally maximal resemblance" (RESCHER 1975: 104). Nevertheless, in answering his own question, Rescher arrives at another question directly connected with the very nature of Lewis' system: How can a theory that is supposed to be alternative to TWI deal with the phenomenon of trans-world travels? Clearly, his criticism expressed in this question is aimed at Lewis' belief that our counterparts could have been us if our world were different. Rescher consequently wonders: "Why should we say of a *merely resembling* individual in another world (even one that is maximally similar) that 'had things been otherwise I would have been him'?" (105).

It should be emphasised that Rescher's critique of Lewis' system represents only one of a vast array of disagreements with Lewis' perspective. Kripke, in his critique of Lewis' conception (which he interprets as a theory identifying objects in possible worlds as identical whenever they are identical in their essential qualities[8]) observes that: "Some may equate the important properties with those properties used to identify the object in the actual world. Surely, these notions are incorrect" (KRIPKE 1980: 76–77). The difference between important and essential qualities is stipulated as follows: "*Important* properties of an object need not be essential, unless 'importance' is used as a synonym for essence, and an object

---

8   Here I wish to express my personal opinion that Saul Kripke misunderstood the fact that Lewis had tried to develop an alternative to TWI, not its substitution.

could have had properties we use to identify it" (77). Another logician, Plantinga, points out the paradoxes to which Lewis' theory leads and which are of a metaphysical nature: "We must therefore conclude, I believe, that Counterpart Theory (taken as a sober metaphysics) affords no real remedy for the ills besetting the Theory of Worldbound Individuals" (PLANTINGA 1974: 120). From a different point of view, Tichý, who strongly objects (as indicated) to mistaking possible worlds for states of affairs, offers us a thorough analysis of Lewis' counterpart theory and directs our attention to its close connection with Lewis' view of possible worlds as a totality of things and an indexical delimitation of the actual world. According to Tichý, Lewis thus challenges the very nature of necessary and accidental: Lewis' "worlds are *disjoint* classes of things" (TICHÝ 1988, 179), which do not contain the same entities, but rather entities that can be similar. Tichý considers this to be the most problematic point of Lewis' theory: How can we speak about possible worlds when, according to Lewis, the only world which can serve as a basis for their construction is our actual world, and thus all its possibilities are expressible through this basis? "One cannot help wondering, incidentally, how we should understand, according to Lewis, the sentence 'It is possible for Reagan to be one inch further to the right.' Should we take it to mean that there is a possible world in which Reagan's counterpart is one inch to the right from Reagan, our worldmate? This would hardly sit happily with Lewis's thesis that inhabitants of distinct worlds are spatially unrelated. Should we take it to mean that there is a possible world where Reagan's counterpart is one inch to the right from himself?" (180).

4. Possible worlds and the actual world

As we can observe at this point, most theorists when speaking about possible worlds use the actual world as an important tool for making their points about possible worlds—all the suggestions are centred around the notion of existence. If possible worlds are ways in which a world could have existed, a question arises: What exactly is the relation between the possible world in question and the actual one—the one which we consider the world of our reality, to which we refer in our everyday experience, in cognition, and in the natural sciences? If we accept this question as relevant we can answer it, broadly speaking, in two different ways: a) the actual world is only one of all possible worlds, and is of the same ontological status as all the other worlds: it does not essentially differ from other possible worlds and is not excluded from their set; b) the actual world is exceptional among other possible worlds—its ontological status is exceptional and other possible worlds are connected with this world only via a relation of resemblance, if they are connected at all.

A) the actual world is one of a number of possible worlds

If we accept this hypothesis immediately we have to face the following issue: Which one from the set of possible worlds is the actual one? Answers to this question differ with regard whether we accept that we are able to distinguish this world from others or not.

i) the actual world is indistinguishable from other possible worlds

With respect to this issue, Tichý suggested that when one wants to keep the validity of basic logical laws and operations, it is impossible in principle to achieve any result other than knowing which world is the actual one: "A property, we know, is a function mapping possible worlds into classes. Hence to specify a class by way of a property one must cite, besides the property itself, a definite world. […] But there is no difficulty here. For it is obviously understood that the requisite world is the *actual* one, the one which actually obtains. But which particular world *is* the actual one? Do we know? To determine which one of the vast range of conceivable worlds is actualised seems to be the ultimate object of science. Whether this object is attainable or not, we can rest assured that it has not been attained yet. All we have (hopefully) achieved so far is to set some of the worlds aside as definitely unactual. But of those that remain *any* – for all we know – may be the actual one. It is easy to see that knowing which possible world is actualised is tantamount to omniscience. For someone who knows the identity of the actual world can readily determine the actual truth value of any given proposition (i.e., a function from possible worlds to truth values) by simply taking the value of the proposition at that world. Now this is certainly not a position we can assume ourselves to be in. But then we must concede that we do not know which world is actual" (TICHÝ 1975: 90–91).

The value of Tichý's approach lies not only in its revelation that it is impossible in principle to distinguish between the actual world and other worlds, but also in his explanation of what the label 'the actual world' really refers to: "The actual world, in other words, is a world-in-intension, i.e., a function, call it '@', taking possible worlds to possible worlds. The value of @ at a world W is the world which is actual in W. And it is easy enough to see which world is actual in a given world W: W itself. @ is thus seen to be the identity function defined on the family of possible worlds. And this function – something we are perfectly familiar with – is what the term 'the actual world' stands for" (TICHÝ 1975: 91). Pavel Materna, following Tichý's reasoning, comes to a similar conclusion in more accessible terms: "*we never can say which of the possible worlds is the actual one. An intuitive* reason is rather simple: If a possible world is a collection of possible facts, then the actual world is the collection of actual facts. To know which of the possible worlds is the actual one means, therefore, to know all actual facts" (MATERNA 1998: 26).

Another strong criticism of distinguishability of the actual world from all possible ones is articulated by Plantinga: possible worlds are inseparably bound to the logical form of a proposition. Indeed, Plantinga's possible worlds are nothing more than what can be said about them. In order to distinguish between possible worlds and the actual one, Plantinga introduces the term, *the book on a world*: "The book on a world W is the set of propositions *true in* W" (PLANTINGA 1974: 46). For Plantinga too the actual world is not essentially different from other possible worlds. The difference between these two types of worlds can, according to Plantinga, only be based only on truth-values of their propositions: proposition p is true in a world W when it is not possible that W is actual and p is not true; therefore, every possible proposition is true in at least one world. Consequently, Plantinga connects propositions with the above mentioned term *book (of a world)*: "for each possible proposition *p* there is at least one book of which it is a member and at least one state of affairs S such that if S had been actual, *p* would have been true" (49). In other words, the actual world is a world in which a certain proposition is true.

ii) the actual possible world is indistinguishable from other possible worlds
One of the best known systems developed around this precondition is again offered by Lewis, who considers the term 'actual world' to refer to one particular indexically demarcable subset of the set of all possible worlds: "Our actual world is only one world among others. We call it alone actual not because it differs in kind from all the rest but because it is the world we inhabit." In his next step, Lewis offers a means of exclusion of the actual world from the set of all possible worlds: "'Actual' is indexical, like 'I' or 'here', or 'now': it depends for its reference on the circumstances of utterance, to wit the world where the utterance is located" (LEWIS 1973: 85). Lewis' conception of the term actual world is, as seen, purely indexical: the actual world is a result of one indexical statement.– this fact actually makes Barbara Partee conclude that Lewis believes "not only that other possible worlds do not differ in kind from the actual world, but that each possible world is just as actual from the point of view of its inhabitants as ours from ours" (PARTEE 1989: 102).

Once more, Lewis' suggestion caused a strong wave of criticism on the part of several prominent logicians. All the critiques share one important idea: an indexical demarcation of the actual world from the set of all possible worlds is, with regard to the notion of a possible world, impossible. Let us briefly mention the most discordant of these voices.

Not surprisingly, one of the strongest reservations towards Lewis' system is, again, raised by Tichý: "Yet there seems a world of difference between 'this', 'now', 'here', 'I', 'you' and the like on the one hand, and 'the actual world' on the other. By pointing this index finger at an object and saying 'this', a speaker directly selects a definite item in his environment and makes it perfectly clear to himself and to his audience precisely *which* particular item is being spoken of. The same goes for 'I', 'now' and other indexical terms. By saying 'the actual world', on the other hand, one is not selecting a particular world. What one directly brings up for consideration is a certain idiosyncratic *feature* – actuality. This feature is bound to be had by some world or other but one leaves it, as it were, to the hard facts to decide which particular world it is" (TICHÝ 1975: 92).

Rescher, in reaction to Lewis' suggestions, finds the most problematic part of the theory to be that which refers to the entity considered to be 'our world' by different inhabitants of the actual world: "But this position fails to give due heed to one significant fact: one must 'begin from where one is', and WE are placed within this actual world of ours. There is no psychical access to other possible worlds from this one. *For us,* other possible worlds remain intellectual projections. Doubtless, these worlds are (or can be projected to be) such that *from their* perspective our world (*the* actual one, since 'the actual' like 'the present' place or time has its egocentric aspect) has the status of an intellectual projection from *their* perspective. But this alters the fact that they are and must be accepted by us as projections from the perspective of *this*, the only perspective in whose terms any discussions of *ours* is *inevitable*: it is not a matter of overcoming some capriciously adopted and in principle alterable point of departure" (RESCHER 1985: 92).

Maxwell John Cresswell brings to the debate an argument that is similar to Rescher's point of view, but Cresswell's possible worlds are, like Plantinga's, strictly bound to the logical form of a proposition. This precondition determines the relationship between the actual world and possible ones: "Possible worlds are ways of the world might have been but isn't. Or rather, among all possible worlds there is only one, the actual world, which is the way the world is" (CRESSWELL 1988: 1). Nevertheless, even this exclusivity is stated very carefully with regard to possible problems of which one should beware: "Possible worlds are things we can talk about or imagine, suppose, believe in or wish for. We can never though ever get to a possible world which is not the real world [...] This is because the real world means the totality of what actually happens [...] When we say that a world is the real world, we are of course speaking from the point of view of our own world. And a person in another possible world who speaks about the 'real world' of course means his world not ours. This is exactly parallel to the way we use the word *now*" (4). As we can see at the very end of this section, Cresswell's reasoning ultimately supports Tichý's as well as Rescher's objections to Lewis' counterpart theory.[9] Nevertheless, this fact does not decrease the value of Lewis' logic for uncovering the relationships between possible worlds – the actual one and fictional worlds, as we will see shortly.

B) the actual world is distinguishable from the set of all possible worlds and is essentially different from other members of this set

Raymond Bradley and Norman Swartz belong to the group of logicians who exclude the actual world from the set of possible worlds. According to their work, actual possible worlds differ from non-actual ones at three levels: a) actual and non-actual possible worlds differ due to the qualities of the objects they encompass; b) non-actual possible worlds contain objects that do not occur in actual possible worlds; c) objects that occur in actual possible worlds are missing in non-actual ones. Whereas the actual world is the world of our reality and is therefore spatially and temporarily determined, non-actual possible worlds do not belong to any physical universe: "Now it is clear that the actual world is a possible world. If something actually exists then it is obviously possible that it exists. On the other hand, not every thing that possibly exists does so actually. Not all possible worlds are actual. It follows, therefore, that the actual world is only one among many possible worlds: that there are possible worlds other than ours. Moreover, given that by 'the actual world' we mean – as we agreed a moment ago – every thing that was, is, or will be the case, it follows that by 'another possible world' we do not mean some planet, star or whatnot that actually exists and which is located somewhere 'out there' in physical space. Whatever actually exists, it must be remembered, belongs to the actual world even if it is light-years away. Other, non-actual possible worlds are not located anywhere in physical space. They are located, as it were, in conceptual space" (BRADLEY-SWARTZ 1979: 5).

Not surprisingly, one of the most striking suggestions about the relationship between possible worlds and the actual one comes from Kripke who, with his

---

9   It seems that Wolfgang Heydrich adopts a similar approach when pointing out the claims of modal realism: "According to modal realism worlds are chunks of reality, maximal individuals, spatio-temporally and causally unconnected with each other. Ontologically, all of them are on a par. No actual world is separated from merely possible ones; with actuality being essentially an indexical concept each world is the actual one according to itself" (HEYDRICH 1989: 188).

well-known, strictly logical rigidity, refers to the specific status of the actual world within a system of logical semantics: "The 'actual world' – better, the actual state, or history of the world – should not be confused with the enormous scattered object that surrounds us. The latter might also have been called 'the (actual) world', but it is not the relevant object here. Thus the possible but not actual worlds are not phantom duplicates of the 'world' in this other sense" (KRIPKE 1980: 19–20). Kripke does not examine the relation between possible worlds and the real one, but simply claims that they are two different entities of different statuses: qualities attributed to the objects of the actual world with respect to their identification have nothing in common with the objects of possible worlds. Therefore, logical semantists, basing their criteria of identity on the essential properties of objects, can actually speak about identity across possible worlds "without worry" (KRIPKE 1980: 51).

At the conclusion of this section, let us mention (once again) the unique and specific conception of the relationship between possible worlds and the actual one suggested by Rescher. In his system, the actual world serves as some kind of base for possible individuals – the actual world always *precedes* the possible one: "On our constructive approach to possible worlds, it is enough to specify the merely descriptive phylogeny of their membership; the ontogenesis implicit in their (conceptual) extraction from the actual is also to be taken as an essential aspect of 'what makes things the things they are.' Thus possible worlds – like the possible individuals that populate them – are defined relative to the actual world as basis (or at any rate relative to a hypothetical actual world – a possible world *assumed* to be actual)" (RESCHER 1985: 90).

5. Possible worlds and truth values

As stated above, a truth valuation of particular propositions is, in the realm of possible worlds, always related to a particular possible world. Possible worlds as logical entities are sets of propositions and the truth value of a proposition can be assigned only within a particular universe of propositions: "any facts (or at least any empirical text) can be construed as a proposition: it can be true or false, depending on possible worlds and time points" (MATERNA 1998: 27). It is obvious that any two possible worlds can differ in the way that, whereas in one of them a particular proposition is true, the same proposition is false in the other. This dichotomy leads Plantinga to the suggestion that "every possible proposition is true in at least one world" (PLANTINGA 1974: 49). Thus, truth valuation in the field of possible worlds semantics always necessarily gains the two values of true and false in particular relation to possible worlds.

In the realm of possible worlds the concept of truth valuation is strongly connected with two other areas of possible world enquiry: a) necessity vs. possibility and b) the trans-worlds-accessibility relation.

5.1 Necessity and possibility

The two-value truth valuation in possible worlds semantics divides the universe containing propositions into two sets that correspond with the basic modal dichotomy of possibility and necessity: a proposition that is true in all possible worlds is necessarily true, whereas a proposition that is only true in one possible world is possibly true. In other words, the necessary is true in all cases, but the possible is true only in some cases. Therefore, it is true that "In the possible worlds logics a statement is true-in-a-world rather than just true" (GIRLE 2000: 35).

5.2 The accessibility-relation between possible worlds

Partee postulates that every model of propositional modal logic necessarily consists of a set of possible worlds W, of a relation of accessibility between the worlds R, and of the truth valuation of every atomic statement in every possible world. In addition, she notes that various accessibility relations correspond to various axiomatic bases for logical systems. Nevertheless, the accessibility relation between possible worlds is commonly defined on the basis of truth valuation: "The accessibility relation between worlds is used to express the idea of a world being possible relative to a world. To say that world u is possible relative to world v (or that u is accessible from v) is to say that every proposition true in u is possible in v" (CHIHARA 1998: 10).

If the accessibility-relation between possible worlds is defined in this manner, it relates to the notions of necessarily and possibly true: "A proposition is necessarily true in a given world if it is true in every world accessible to that world" (HUGHES-CRESSWELL 1968: 77). Nevertheless, for the purposes of this study, we can rely on the fact that particular qualities of the accessibility relation are determined by its truth valuation basis.

6. Possible worlds and linguistics

The essential questions raised by many linguists and logicians are whether any logical systems exist that can be used for a logic analysis of natural language; and if so, which ones are the proper ones. When answering this question, the majority of scholars come to a definite conclusion: "Although simplification, idealisation and reduction are inevitable in any process of theory formation and especially in formalization, the use of logical models may not obscure relevant linguistic facts. The use of classical propositional and predicate calculi often obscured the role of such important linguistic categories as articles, adverbs, conjunctions, mood, time, aspect, etc. and often neglected the hierarchical structure of the syntax of the sentences represented. The introduction of the more powerful (i.e., precisely 'weak' and 'flexible') modal systems obviously has greater promises for linguistic description" (van DIJK 1973: 160–161). This suggestion actually refers to something seemingly evident from the very beginning of this chapter: a general dissatisfaction with the possible use of predicate logic for describing a natural language, leading to the development of various alternative conceptions.

From this perspective many scholars have focused on the applicability of these new, alternative conceptions to the issue of natural language. Nevertheless, when doing so they have had to follow some presumptions. The first presumption, which emphasises the diverse and unrelated backgrounds of logical and linguistic approaches, is formulated explicitly by François Rastier: "Indeed, languages and many texts are not subject to the so called laws of thought that are the principle of identity, the excluded third and non-contradiction. With certain exceptions, textual worlds are open worlds, that is to say that the denotation of their graphs can be undefined or inconsistent. Besides, at least for a given interpretation, these worlds are *finite*" (RASTIER 1990: 54–55). For the purposes of this study, two moments within Rastier's reasoning seem especially crucial. First, language material is already given and logical systems can be only applied to it from above; thus textual universes differ from logical universes constructed from below. Language universes can be "inspected by powerful telescopes." Secondly, textual universes are finite because they are expressed by finite texts – this seems to be a breaking point for further analyses of fictional worlds. A formulation of the same conviction, although in different terms, is also provided by another linguist, Teun van Dijk: "The use of logical models in present-day linguistics is extensive but has not been without methodological problems. Like for all formal models, it is necessary to be clearly aware of the fact that we have to represent linguistic structures not logical structures" (van DIJK 1973: 160).[10]

As we can see, van Dijk's suggestion is especially valuable in formulating a methodological basis for any analysis undertaken in this field; however, it does not bring us closer to the concept of possible worlds of linguistics. Rastier

---

10 Van Dijk, in his analyses, displays the full range of his scepticism with regard to the possibility of logical formalisation on natural language's structures (cf. van DIJK 1973: 161).

further specifies the differences of both structures: "Modal logics that have proliferated since the twenties are extremely interesting for linguists [...], for whom Boolean logic readily loses its satisfaction. However, to my knowledge, except in partial or contrived examples, none of them can be applied systematically to the description of languages. This is because the plasticity of natural languages makes it impossible to reduce them to formal languages. Their signs are neither constant nor variable, and they are modified unpredictably as they occur, both at the level of expression and of content. It is up to logic to accommodate itself to language if it can, and not for linguistics to set its descriptions on existing logic" (RASTIER: 53).

To apply possible worlds to language structures actually means to examine how essentially linguistic structures; such as, possible worlds structures are "imposed." Partee shows how efficient this procedure really is: "I would summarize the kinds of possible-worlds theories have had for linguistic semantics as being of two kinds: (i) possible worlds as a technical tool have helped to provide an appropriate *structure* on the space of meanings; (ii) as a further benefit, not so much within linguistics proper but of potential value for linking linguistics to other disciplines, the possible worlds conception is of great help in relating linguistic meaning to other kinds of informational content" (PARTEE 1989: 108). At this point, it is important that when applying possible worlds to linguistic universes we obtain a broader space for the analysis of universes that are based on language and are, in fact, already given: fictional worlds.

6.1 Cresswell's possible worlds and natural language

M. J. Cresswell's theoretical approach seems particularly relevant to the ultimate aim of this study in that it is based on natural language analyses and strives to describe natural language by means of possible worlds semantics. Cresswell's attitude towards linguistic entities is atomistic – it is accommodated at the level of lexis and seeks logical counterparts for linguistic structures. The author examines particular terms in the logical semantics of possible worlds for the purpose of analysing specific statements assigned as propositional attitudes. Cresswell extends his system of semantics in order to analyse any statement in natural language.

Cresswell's possible worlds are theoretical entities given through language: languages are essential preconditions for any possible world's representation. Nevertheless, here we are dealing with natural language, which does not construct any system formalised for the purposes of logic. Natural language exists prior to all formalised systems: communication simply precedes logic. "Language then becomes a rule-governed device for putting into the mind of another a representation of the same set of possible worlds which is in the mind of the speaker. If this is so then the notion of a possible world is at the heart of semantics, and is even more basic than the notion of truth" (CRESWELL 1988: 29). Consequently, Cresswell himself tries to formulate the specificity of such an attitude and to distinguish the motivation leading towards it from that of formal logic: "In actually using a language, in many cases we do not say exactly what we mean or do not mean what we literally say; often, even, there is no exact thing that we mean. Formal theories of meaning idealize from this messy state of affairs. They assume that words have precise and definite meanings and then sentences are understood literally. The hope, of course, is that beginning with a theory of meaning of this idealized kind, one can then use it as the basis of a model of actual language use" (CRESSWELL 1985: 5).

As indicated above, Cresswell builds his system around the notion of propositional attitudes – specific statements of the following type: "Xenia told me that $8 + 3 = 15$" (CRESSWELL 1985: 14). Further, the author suggests that propositional attitudes are touchstones of a more complex issue of truth valuation in possible worlds semantics. The author starts with the claim that a semantics that reflects only the reference of statements and does not consider their structure (a semantics based not on extension of statements but on their intension) arrives at a problematic point: "The problem of propositional attitudes arises in the following way. If the meaning of a sentence is just the set of worlds in which the sentence is true, then any two sentences that are true in exactly the same set of worlds must have the same meaning, or in other words must express the same proposition. Therefore, if a person takes any attitude (for instance, belief) to the proposition expressed by one of those sentences, then that person must take the same attitude to the proposition expressed by the other" (CRESSWELL 1985: 4). When we follow the presumption that Cresswell's possible worlds are sets of propositions that are linguistic entities, it is clear that the only way to analyse propositional attitudes is to examine the linguistic qualities and structures of the propositions. Therefore, Cresswell re-introduces the notion of *sense*, which is dependent on the structure of a given proposition: "The sense of an expression consists, roughly, of the meanings of the parts of that expression combined in a structure that reflects the structure of the sentence" (78).

It would be highly interesting at this point to examine the whole of Cresswell's analysis of propositional attitudes in detail; however, it is important to emphasise that, on the one hand, his approach legitimises possible worlds semantics for the purpose of formal semantics of propositional attitudes in particular, but on the other, it offers ways in which possible worlds semantics can be used for the semantic analysis of natural language in general. By elaborating on the particular preconditions of the use of propositional attitudes and by demonstrating the relationship between both kinds of semantics, Cresswell offers tools for connecting possible worlds semantics with larger linguistic universes, of which literary texts are a part.

To conclude this section, let me offer a comment on Cresswell's view of truth valuation in his possible worlds semantics. From the foregoing discussion, it is clear that Cresswell considers possible worlds as already given (existing) entities: first, there are languages, statements, and communication; their analysis then comes second. Thus Cresswell, in contrast to traditional possible worlds attitudes, does not see possible worlds as atomistic entities constructed from below; his possible worlds can be viewed as comprehensive language universes, not formal constructs. Nevertheless, defining possible worlds in Cresswell's manner causes new and specific problems evaded by formal logic and its rigid atomism. The most striking of these are the issues of TWI and truth valuation: Cresswell's possible worlds are not solely constructed to contain either a proposition A or its negation ¬A, which is necessary for all logically consistent universes; there exist statements which are, within these worlds, "undecidable" (CRESSWELL 1988: 7).

7. Extension and intension

7.1 Basic logical terms

To begin this section, it will be useful to provide a brief review of logical terms essential to this area of research.

The first important terminological distinction is connected with logic as a discipline: that of distinguishing between two basic trends grounded in different attitudes toward the object of examination – classic logic (non-modal, extensional) vs. non-classic logic (non-extensional), the latter with its subtypes of modal and intensional logic.

Classic (extensional) logic can be demarcated by two essential principles: it is two-valued, i.e., truth valuation works only with the values true and false; and, more importantly, it is based on the extensional principle, which requires that only the extension of particular statements can be logically expressed – it is restricted to an actual world and fixed time. In other words, a truth valuation is determined by the state of the world to which the statement refers and which it describes at a specific time.

When I say that classic logic is based on the extensional principle I should emphasise what we understand by the term extension (of a statement): the extension of a statement is the statement's referent, its scope, i.e., an object or a set of objects to which the statement refers in the actual world, that of our reality.

By contrast, non-extensional logic is developed as an alternative to classic logic in order to bypass disadvantages involved in classic logic, which, as all highly formalised systems, has its own limits when it comes to interpreting systems that are not well formalised. Logic of this type can be used primarily for the logical interpretation of natural language.

7.2 Gottlob Frege

Gottlob Frege, who is considered the founder of modern logical semantics, in the first part of his article *Über Sinn und Bedeutung* (1892) introduces the terms *Sinn* and *Bedeutung*, which he applies to language expressions. Whereas Bedeutung is usually translated into English as reference, Sinn is the sense of a statement – the two undetachable elements together constitute the meaning of a language expression. In his article, Frege suggests that for a statement's meaning, what is important is not only the object (or set of objects) to which a statement refers, but also the way this object is given to us through a language statement. Thus, Frege's semantics consists of two components, reference and sense; the latter is dependent on the structure of a statement. This idea has proven very fruitful for solving specific problems in predicate logic.

At this point another crucial feature of Frege's system should be considered. Gottlob Frege actually argued that the meaning of a statement is represented by its truth-value. In this respect Jaroslav Peregrin emphasises that Frege actually developed and used his own principle of the replaceability of synonyms, "which stipulates that the identity of the meanings of the parts of two sentences implies the identity of truth values of the sentences and that in every sentence an expression can be replaced by a synonymous expression without a change in truth-value" (PEREGRIN 1998: 13). Nevertheless, a continuous replacement of the synonyms of sentences with equal truth-value leads us to the conclusion "that truth valuation always survives the replacement of expressions with equal extension" (44). This conclusion does not seem to be problematic at first sight, but as Frege himself had already pointed out, contexts in which the replacements of synonyms without changing their truth-values are impossible; he calls these contexts *indirect*. In these contexts, very often sense and truth-values change – mainly for stylistic reasons. This suggestion has essential consequences for an analysis of natural language and leads to the birth of intensional logic.

7.3 Rudolf Carnap

When using the terms *extension* and *intension* I borrow from Rudolf Carnap, who coined them initially. Peregrin explicitly states that "Carnap's thoughts led to the development of what had started to be called intensional logic and what actually meant the ultimate convergence of the semantics of natural language and the theory of formal languages" (PEREGRIN 1998: 22). Indeed, Carnap not only introduced the terms, but also linked them to the logical analysis of natural language from the outset. He explicitly pointed out that the area of symbolic logic, which examines artificially constructed language systems, is just as important as the area of pragmatics, which is connected with the empirical investigation of particular natural languages. The categories of extension and intension are, as we will see shortly, bound in the Carnapian view to an analysis of natural language, and thus particularly relevant to the aims of this book.

The way in which Carnap defines extension, i.e., as a set of individuals to which an expression refers in the actual world, is still widely used.[11] Intension is defined, according to Carnap, as "designative meaning component" (CARNAP 1955: 34). In other words, intension can be understood as a dictionary definition. By defining extension and intension in this way, Carnap actually shows the value the two concepts have for predicate logic: "two predicates are synonymous if and only if they have the same intension" (34). This statement seems to be much more profitable for an analysis of natural language than the classical definition of extensional synonymy, which teaches us that two expressions are synonymous when they refer to the same individual in the actual world. Furthermore, when defining the synonymy of two statements, Carnap introduces the notion of intensional isomorphism. According to this, statements are synonymous when intensions of all the corresponding parts of these expressions are identical.

Carnap further suggests that whereas for the analysis of a particular language a symbolic-logical approach proceeds from the recognition of intensions to the recognition of extensions, a purely logical approach proceeds in the opposite fashion. Nevertheless, he also suggested that for the study of symbolic logic a pragmatic investigation is of special importance due to the fact that the results and empirical concepts of classical linguistics can function within the study of theoretical logical systems. This specific point of view became especially inspirational for those of Carnap's successors who think of logic from a linguistic perspective.

---

11 Quine, similarily to Carnap, defines extension as a set of objects to which a true expression refers (cf. Quine 1967: 65).

Intension, in the Carnapian view, is equal to what the author calls the "cognitive meaning component" (CARNAP 1955: 37): whereas the cognitive meaning component is "relevant for the determination of truth," the non-cognitive element of meaning, which is "irrelevant for questions of truth and logic, may still be very important for the psychological effect of a sentence on a listener, e.g., by emphasis, emotional associations, motivational effects" (37). At this point, we can clearly see why Carnap is considered a direct successor of Gottlob Frege: Carnap replaces the terms of *reference* and *sense* with the notions of *extension* and *intension* and uses them for shaping Frege's original suggestions into a systematic theoretical framework. Carnap modifies the principle of interchangeability of synonyms in order to claim the identical meaning of a statement in all contexts, which actually transfers the priciple from an indirect context to the intensional level. According to this new view, a statement has an identical extension in all contexts; however, the intensions can vary. In this way the contextual elements, which are often of a stylistic nature, are provided with the intensional part of the meaning. Carnap discards Frege's concept of indirect context and replaces it with extensional and intensional contexts. In other words, Carnap reformulates the principle of interchangeability of synonyms for extensions and intensions separetely.[12]

When Carnap investigates the linguistic demarcation of a statement's intension from its extension he literally claims that it is necessary to "take into account not only the actual cases, but also possible cases" and further generalises: "All logically possible cases come into consideration for the determination of intensions" (38). If so, "the intension of a predicate may be defined as its range, which comprehends those possible kinds of objects for which the predicate holds" (39). Carnap is describing a procedure commonly used by linguists in order to detect all possible methods of determining range: "The most direct way of doing this would be for the linguist to use [...] modal expressions corresponding to 'possible case' or the like" (38).

Another idea employed by Carnap in his system, and particularly relevant to the aims of this book, is the concept of *identity*. From the preceding discussion it is obvious that identity must be examined at both levels of meaning – at both extensional and intensional levels. Kutchera, in slightly metaphorical fashion, points out that whereas Carnap's notion of identity of extensions belongs

---

12 Nevertheless, as Franz von Kutschera states, there are contexts which stand outside the set of intensional contexts and they are known as non-*intensional* contexts. An example of a context of this sort can be considered contexts containing the model operator of belief (see Kutschera 1975, pg. 43).

to the field of the empirical, the notion of identity of intensions belongs to the area of linguistics. When Carnap investigates the identity of intensions, he introduces the notion of *intensional isomorphism* as follows: two statements are intensionally isomorphic when intensions of all the corresponding elements are identical. This means that according to Carnap no two expressions with different structures can be identical. As we will see, for the analysis of natural language this statement is of major importance.

From all that has been said about Carnap's contribution, we can infer two important results that lie at the core of modern non-extensional logical systems: a) an intension of the expression, as a part of the expression's meaning, is dependent on the structure of the expression; and b) intensions are detectable in the framework of all logically possible cases. At this point, we are actually only one step from a systematic analysis of the notion of possible worlds in logical semantics.

7.4 Richard Montague

Once Carnap established the link between an analysis of formal logic and the analysis of natural language, it seems to be reasonable to claim that Richard Montague became the main contributor to this kind of semantic thought. On the one hand, Montague shows the connection between the two domains, while on the other, he reserves specific methodologies for each domain. First, Montague claims that both methodologies should inspire each other. He works from the assumption that no essential differences between natural and formal languages can be found and that both can be analysed in similar ways.[13] As a result, we can suggest that Montague's main aim is to undertake a logical analysis of natural language using the devices of formalised logical systems. From the point of view of linguistics, the most important contribution of Montague's work is his attempt to provide a logical analysis of English.

Montague's system for the logical analysis of natural language consists of two parts: grammar and intensional logic. Whereas grammar translates a natural language into a formal one (which lacks semantics), intensional logic translates the formal language into another formal language, which is a language of intensional logic that possesses semantics. Montague's grammar does not split the syntax of natural language from its semantics but, on the contrary, claims that the "idea

---

13 At this point, it is important to state that most logicians (strongly) disagree with this assumption. The most common reservation regarding this assumption comes from the fact that formal languages are *constructed* whereas natural languages are *described* by means of logic.

that the syntax of language is fundamentally connected with the semantics of a language" (ALLWOOD & ANDERSSON & DAHL 1977: 131). It is obvious, at first sight, that this bi-level essence of the analysis of natural language, which is profitable in terms of logical analysis, is too formalised for the purposes of linguistics. This is mainly due to the fact that a translation of one single sentence written in natural language into formalised forms requires several pages of for-malised text. It seems that this particular feature of Richard Montague's analysis resulted not only in the strong criticism expressed by his followers but also poin-ted out the possible pitfalls of complexity in their own approaches.[14]

As stated, Montague's logical system is based on Carnap's assumption that every expression has two dimensions: extension and intension. In order to avoid logically problematic statements, for example those which contain non-existent animals; such as, a unicorn in statements of the type: "John searches for a uni-corn," the author considers the meaning of the expression "unicorn" an intension of the expression, whereas in the statement "John found a unicorn" the meaning of the expression "unicorn" is considered its extension. To put these ideas into more general terms: if possible, the meaning of an expression is considered its extension and in other cases the meaning of an expression is its intension. In any event, according to Montague's semantics (and also according to intensional logic) intension is a function from possible worlds to individuals, i.e., a function that assigns a set of individuals to a particular possible world for which a parti-cular statement is true. In other words, the function assigns a possible world the set of its extensions. In this case the intension of the expression "unicorn" is its extension related to a particular possible world, i.e., an extension, though related to possible worlds.[15] As Peregrin explicitly states, "In this sense Montague's se-mantics stays formally extensional: the meaning is always an extension" (PERE-GRIN 1998: 100). Partee draws a similar conclusion about intensions when she claims, "these *functions* from possible worlds to extensions are still functions in

---

14 Some of them went so far that they later came up with a conclusion that Montague's system actually contains significant imperfections which made it totally unattractive: the main imperfection is considered the specific use of ^operator crucial for his model of intensional logic, which makes the system logically inconsistent.

15 As Barbara Partee similarly argues: "Following the standard treatment of possible-worlds semantics, we take the extension of a sentence to be a truth value, and its intension to be a function from possible worlds to truth values" (PARTEE 1989: 97).

an *extensional* sense: functions completely representable as sets of ordered pairs" (PARTEE 1989: 119).[16]

If so, where does the importance of Montague's revolutionary (though not easily applicable) system for this study actually lie? In order to answer this question, two crucial moments of his system should be emphasised. First, Montague insists on a logically linguistic approach to the analysis of natural language and therefore rejects submitting this analysis fully under the realm of formal language models; he tries to "translate" a natural language into a formal one. The fact that this approach proved complex and was criticised for its formality reveals the very limits of the formal logical analysis of natural language and uncovering these limits is important for the final purpose of this book. Secondly, Montague completely adopted the view of possible worlds as logical constructs with specific qualities – as does Saul Kripke (see below). Therefore, Montague understands this logical concept as a world constructed by a set of statements, i.e., as a purely logical realm in which it is impossible to classify the truth-values of statements that are not implied by the statements from which the possible world is constructed. Montague states that we can find two possible worlds that are indistinguishable in the ways they are expressed through language, but which still can vary: "for example, in that in one [possible world] everyone believes the proposition that snow is white, while in the other someone does not believe it" (MONTAGUE 1974: 154). It seems that at this point that, when claiming that possible worlds actually exist somewhere beyond language, at a higher ontological level and thus beyond the analysis of language, the author actually crosses the borders of logic: according to logic, fictional worlds are by definition specific sets of propositions. Thus, Montague's suggestion does not seem to be of special scholarly value for the purpose of the investigation of possible worlds; however, it does have value for fictional worlds considered to exist beyond the universe of language.

7.5 Saul Kripke

Anyone who strives to understand the concepts of extension and intension in more detail must, at some point, encounter the name of Saul Kripke and his system of possible worlds, which is often considered the main contribution to possible worlds theory. In order to demonstrate the originality of Kripke's solutions of particular problems connected with modal statements, it is important here to focus on the essential qualities of predicate logic.

---

16 From a purely methodological point of view it is obvious that logicians use the term *function* similarly to the ways in which mathematicians use the term *relation*.

In the system of predicate logic, a subject assigns an individual and a predicate a function that distributes truth-values to particular subjects, while a statement assigns a truth-value: "Thus, for example, the name John assigns a man, predicate stupid assigns a function which to every stupid individual assigns the truth-value VERUM and to every individual who is not stupid the truth value FALSUM; the statement John is stupid therefore assigns the truth-value which the function assigns to the individual assigned by the name John" (PEREGRIN 1998: 13). From a semantic point of view, classical predicate logic considers the meaning of a predicate, which represents a function from the universe of individuals to truth-values, to be a subset of the universe of discourse: "The function operating from the universe to truth-values can be always viewed as a demarcation of a certain set: it divides the universe into two sets, to the set of items to which it assigns V and to those to which it assigns F; practically the function isolates the items belonging to the demarcated set from those which do not belong there" (PEREGRIN 1996: 13; see also ALLWOOD-ANDERSSON-DAHL 1977: 22–23). Thus, the meaning of a statement is its truth-value; a statement is true when a subject belongs to a set referred to by the predicate. It is obvious that predicate logic of this kind cannot, for example, deal with an interpretation of modal statements. Kripke therefore reacts to the Carnapian claim of assigning intensions to all logically possible cases and confronts these cases with possible worlds: "To say that something is possible is in fact to say that it is actual in some possible world" (PEREGRIN 1998: 98). Thus, the notion of a logically possible world becomes a central concept in Kripke's system as a whole: "The main and the original motivation for the 'possible world analysis' – and the way it clarified modal logic – was that it enabled modal logic to be treated by the same set theoretic techniques of model theory that proved so successful when applied to extensional logic" (KRIPKE 1980: 19).

What Kripke evaluates as "successful" actually represents a description of his own path. He is the thinker who has added the dimension of possible worlds to extensional predicate logic, or in other words, created a version of predicate logic applicable to possible worlds. In his system of semantics, the meaning of a name is a function that assigns every possible world a subject to which the name in this world refers. The meaning of the predicate is also a function that assigns every possible world the extension of the predicate in this world (or a set of individuals for which the predicate is valid in the world), which implies that the meaning of a predicate is a function from possible worlds to the sets of individuals. Finally, the meaning of a statement is a function that assigns every possible world a truth-value of the statement in this possible world, i.e., it is a function from possible worlds to truth-values. These suggestions imply that this function actually divides all possible worlds into two subsets from which the statement is true in one and false in the other; therefore, the meaning of a statement can be considered a subset of all possible worlds in which the statement is true. In conclusion, it can be said that Kripke's semantics is actually extensional logic semantics enriched by the dimension of possible worlds – as if it had been "run" through all possible worlds.

As we can see, Kripke's modal logic implies that the truth-value of any expression can be decided only with regard to a particular possible world. This identification of the meaning of an expression with a subset of possible worlds is very fruitful especially for a logical analysis of modal aspects of a language; however, for a literary theoretical investigation the path comes to a stop at this point.

II. Fictional worlds as possible worlds

1. Preliminary motivations

Fictional worlds semantics builds to a considerable extent on the notion of possible worlds used by logical semantics. The theory of fictional worlds considers fictional worlds to be specific kinds of possible worlds but, at the same time, fictional worlds are determined by their specific qualities arising from their specific status. The main motivation for employing possible worlds for the purpose of a fictional analysis comes from the intuitive assumption (partly derived from concrete examples provided by the same theoreticians of logical discourse) that both possible as well as fictional worlds remain outside the realm of our actual world and that "fictional worlds are concrete constellations of states of affairs which, like possible worlds, are non-actualized in the world" (RONEN 1994: 51). Nevertheless, the question is whether the intuitively felt similarity between possible and fictional worlds makes it worth adjusting the logical discourse to the fictional, with all the difficulties and problems it may cause, in order to reach a valid analytical tool for examining fictional worlds and their structures. Fortunately, it seems that fictional worlds borrow from possible worlds only when profitable. The main profit fictional worlds semantics gains from logical possible worlds is the referential frame: "Possible worlds hence provide a general framework and context for describing the most notable influence of philosophical discourse on the literary theory of fictionality and they supply the grounds for reorienting literary theory toward questions of reference, ontology and representation" (5). Thomas Pavel goes even further when connecting the use of logical discourse for the purpose of a fictional one with the fictional world's own typology. The latter being, in his view, crucial for fictional semantics: "rather than a rigorously unified semantics, fiction needs a typology of worlds to represent the variety of fictional practice. And if, on the one hand, technically impeccable possible worlds are too narrowly defined to provide for a model in the theory of fiction, on the other hand the notion of world as an ontological metaphor for fiction remains too appealing to be dismissed" (PAVEL 1986: 50).

Generally speaking, fictional worlds are viewed as specific structures generated by fictional texts, to which all the entities founded by fictional texts are ultimately related. These entities are of the same ontological status: they exist fictionally.[17] "Fictional worlds of literature [...] are a special kind of possible worlds; they are aesthetic artefacts constructed, preserved, and circulating in the medium of fictional texts [...] Since they are constructed by semiotic systems – language, colours, shapes, tones, acting, and so on – we are justified in calling them semiotic objects" (DOLEŽEL 1998: 15–16). Fictional worlds come into existence in a specific *semiotic process*, which serves to detach them from the set of other worlds. Ruth Ronen, in her general examination of fictional existence, indicates those elements particularly significant to the investigation of fictional discourse:

1. That fictional discourse can create or construct the objects to which it refers.
2. That fictional discourse can create or construct incomplete but well in-dividuated objects (incompleteness does not contradict the self-identity of entities).
3. That fiction can construct impossible objects and other objects that clearly diverge from their counterparts in the actual world" (RONEN 1994: 45).

2. Possible worlds of logic and fiction

It is obvious that the possible worlds of logical calculus cannot simply be trans-ferred to another field of semantic investigation, including fictional worlds se-mantics, without major adjustments to make them compatible with the specific needs of the field to which they are applied. Possible worlds are, above all, inter-pretative models for logical statements of a certain type, which could not be in-terpreted without this framework; therefore, possible worlds in logical discourse serve primarily as a tool for modal logic.[18] By contrast, possible worlds of fiction (fictional worlds) serve as referential frames for entities based in fictional texts and are not, in themselves, formalised logical models for analyses of fictional texts; rather, they represent specific structures composed of fictional individuals, which can be viewed and interpreted in the context of those worlds. The basic difference between the two kinds of worlds lies in the ways in which they come into existence: whereas possible worlds are built from below as sets of statements

---

17 Many philosophers and theoreticians deny fictional entities' existence. For example Nicolas Wolterstorff explicitly states that fictional characters "don't exist" (WOLTER-STORFF 1980: 135).

18 Ruth Ronen, however, strictly points out that fictional worlds do not serve this purpose within fictional discourse – due to the fact that fictional worlds are simply not modal extensions of the actual one (cf. RONEN 1994: 87).

acting as referential frames for logical universes, fictional worlds are based on fictional texts and activated by the readers of those texts. It seems that when Saul Kripke metaphorically states that possible worlds cannot be observed with some form of powerful telescope, he is referring exactly to this difference. Similarly, Ruth Ronen claims that philosophers reject the idea that possible worlds could exist in space and time (see RONEN 1994: 50).

If we use the above mentioned Kripke's metaphor for the realm of fictional worlds, we can say that fictional worlds can be observed by some powerful telescopes – especially due to the fact that fictional texts always refer to a set of fictional facts that can in some sense be viewed through some form of semantic code. In this sense fictional worlds are closer to certain kinds of semiotic landscapes than to interpretative models for possible worlds or sets of propositions. Thomas Pavel, when elaborating on the relationship between these two kinds of worlds, uses Saul Kripke's metaphor: "Usually philosophers assume that possible worlds are not genuine concrete entities that could be inspected were we to possess the adequate telescope; they are abstract models, and may be thought of either as actual abstract entities or as conceptual constructions. But if so, the relation between a world and its creator matters less; to represent works of fiction as worlds involves a model that does not necessarily include a rigorous theory of the production of the fictional world" (PAVEL 1986: 49). Umberto Eco, who also has significally contributed to the final shape of fictional worlds theory, proceeds from the idea of furnished worlds that are obviously visible – with or without telescopes: "On the contrary, it seems evident that in the framework of narrative analysis, either one considers given *furnished* and nonempty worlds or there will be no difference between a fiction theory and logic of counterfactuals" (ECO 1990: 65).

As observed at the beginning of this chapter, Ruth Ronen claims that fictional worlds are, like the possible worlds of logical semantics, sets of non-actualised states of affairs. In this respect fictional worlds share one important characteristic with possible worlds: potentially they are infinite in number. As sets of non-actualised states of affairs, fictional worlds are granted to be potentially infinite in number – but of course, only if there were an infinite number of fictional texts that could generate them.

Nevertheless, fictional worlds are also considerably restricted: they are comprised of a finitude number of individuals and objects. This restriction does not apply to possible worlds of logical semantics ad definitio – possible worlds are infinite in number from their own essence, from the way in which they are constructed. Possible worlds are maximal sets of affairs (statements) that correspond with all the ways in which a world could have been. As Nicolas Wolterstorff explicitly states, whereas possible worlds are possible states of affairs which "are *maximally comprehensive*, fictional worlds are not" (WOLTERSTORFF 1980: 131). Maximality of this kind is definitely not congruous with fictional worlds, since they are generated through the medium of finite fictional texts, which place them under strong restrictions. They are not universes of all possible states of affairs (statements) anymore, but rather states of affairs "allowed" by fictional texts.

Now, let us introduce a simple personal example. I can definitely imagine a possible world in which my father has not been a ceramicist but a sailor. This statement (false in the actual world) is true with regard to a particular possible world in which the statement is congruous with other statements of the world. In this case a statement "My father is a sailor" can be true in an infinite number of possible worlds, whereas in the actual world it is false. Similarly, a statement that Little Dorrit of Charles Dickens' famous novel of that title was a sailor is false with regard to the fictional world based on Dickens' novel. To find a fictional world in which this statement is true means to write a different fictional text.

Being accommodated in fictional texts, fictional worlds are necessarily incomplete – simply because they are based in finite fictional texts. Therefore, it is possible to imagine that Little Dorrit at some point meets Christopher Ward, a real watch-maker of the actual world, who makes her a special discount automatic-watch offer. However, Christopher Ward is not mentioned at any moment in the flow of the Dickens story. Furthermore, there are no markers in the world of Dickens' novel from which we can infer the existence of such a watch-maker – and there is no cognitive procedure which would justify this existence. Due to this specific quality of incompleteness of fictional worlds, literary theoreticians, in order to characterise fictional worlds, use Umberto Eco's (1990) term "small worlds."[19] Small worlds are by definition worlds obtaining finite sets of individuals and parameters, and therefore fictional worlds, which are "macrostructures ('mereological sums') constituted by a finite number of possible particulars," can be considered small worlds (DOLEŽEL 1998: 15).[20]

---

19 The term was originally used by Jaakko Hintikka (1983); similarily Saul Kripke (1980) offers the term *miniworld*. Umberto Eco re-defined this term for the purpose of literary studies.

20 Jaakko Hintikka suggested the term *semantics of possible situations* to replace *small worlds* which necessarily are not cosmologies or world histories (cf. HINTIKKA 1983: 153). This semantics of possible situations is according to the author de facto a theory of situations.

2.1 Impossible worlds

The term impossible world seems to be understood from an intuitive point of view to all of us. Nevertheless, impossible worlds are clearly and rigidly defined within the realm of possible worlds that are logically *consistent*, logically *complete*, and controlled by logical *implication*. Any world that disturbs at least one of the three qualities is impossible.

It is obvious that in the fictional world discourse the requirement of logical completeness is irrelevant. Simply, not all statements about a fictional world can be provided with truth-values. This fact is a necessary result in the fictional world's quality of incompleteness. There are many statements that can be articulated about a fictional world but we are not able to say whether they are true or false with regard to the world. A fictional text founding the world can give us not enough information to decide; the text may just be silent: "only some conceivable statements about fictional entities are decidable, while some are not" (DOLEŽEL 1998: 22). Let us use an example from another famous work of literature, Franz Kafka's *Metamorphosis* (1915), which starts with the well known sentence: "When Gregor Samsa awoke one morning from troubled dreams he found himself transformed in his bed into a monstrous insect" (KAFKA 2000:76). At this very moment Gregor starts communicating with the other members of the family, who want to make him wake up and go to work, through his bedroom door. Therefore, the communication involves only "invisible" voices. Whereas the mother's voice is described as *gentle* and Gregor's as *intermingled*, both referring to certain sound qualities, the voice of Gregor's father is described as becoming *deeper* during the conversation (a comparative quality) and finally the sister's voice is assigned *no quality* at all. If so, the reader cannot employ any procedure that would bring him closer to the quality of the sister's voice. There is no access to this knowledge, neither directly, nor through any implicative move.

The fact of the existence of non-decidable qualities in fiction is strongly connected to another quality of possible worlds not transferable to fictional worlds: it seems to be more than problematic to bind fiction with the axiom of truth-valuation (which is intertwined with the process of logical implication within the realm of possible worlds): "Literary texts, like most informal collections of sentences, such as conversations, newspaper articles, eyewitness testimony, history books, biographies of famous people, myths, and literary criticism, display a property that may puzzle logicians but that doubtless appears natural to anyone else: their truth as a whole is not recursively definable starting from the truth of the individual sentences that constitute them. Global truth is not simply derived from the local truth-value of the sentences present in the text"

(PAVEL 1986: 17). If so, the result of the implication procedure in fiction stays ambiguous – if we cannot truth valuate particular statements, neither can we truth-valuate the statement implied by these statements.[21] Thus, the question is: Is it possible to speak about truth-valuation and fiction at the same time? If so, how can this be achieved? The answers to these questions vary. Nicolas Wolterstorff, for example, excludes fiction from truth-valuation completely: "Corresponding to these two different concepts of world are the two distinct concepts of *being true in* (some possible world) and *being included within* (some work's world)" (WOLTERSTORFF 1980: 134). Terence Parsons, on the other hand, allows fiction a certain kind of truth-valuation: "as the reader reads, an account is constructed by extrapolation from the sentences being read. The account is modified and expanded during the reading, and the final result may be called the *maximal account*. Then what is true in the story is just whatever the maximal account explicitly says, and nothing else" (PARSONS 1999: 175). While Parson's offer initially sounds very restrictive, it seems that it does actually subsume all the possibilities that can be assigned as true in fiction – in other words, the truth in fiction depends on the fictional text.

The final quality mentioned in connection with the essential axioms of possible worlds of logical discourse was logical consistency. It is clear that, especially in modern fiction, we can encounter many examples of violations of this axiom. Among others, Lubomír Doležel exemplifies this phenomenon by O. Henry's short story *Roads of Destiny* in which the main character actually dies three times in three different ways; this is a telling example of the violation of logical consistency.

The example above indicates the final result that fictional worlds do not or cannot fulfil the first two axioms of logical possible worlds and, additionally, some of them do not fulfil even the third one. Thomas Pavel states: "Works of fiction more or less dramatically combine incompatible world-structures, play with the impossible, and incessantly speak about the unspeakable" (PAVEL 1986: 62). This fact is the most telling evidence for fiction not to be "strictly identified with metaphysically possible worlds" (48).

As has been said, fictional worlds cannot by definition fulfil the first two axioms of possible worlds and only some fulfil the third. This fact makes the

---

21 Maria-Laure Ryan surprisingly suggests that a world is possible when it is not contradictory and fulfils the law of the excluded middle (see RYAN 1991: 31). However, it seems that not all the axioms of logically possible worlds can be narrowed down to these two preconditions; on top of that, the law of excluded middle is a subset of the precondition of logical consistence.

third axiom interesting for further investigation, mainly because it splits fictional worlds into two incongruent subsets: those which fulfil the axiom and those which do not. Indeed, fictional worlds theory distinguishes between possible and impossible worlds: "Contradictory objects nevertheless provide insufficient evidence against the notion of *world*, since nothing prevents the theory of fiction from speaking, as some philosophers do, about impossible or erratic worlds" (PAVEL 1986: 49). These fictional worlds are not only imaginable but also often practiced in modern prose. Therefore, the notion of an impossible possible world, within fictional discourse, is not only relevant but also profitable in terms of a fictional worlds typology.

With regard to quality of finitude, fictional worlds are in strict opposition to possible worlds and also to the actual one. This opposition is founded at the very origin of fictional worlds and in their epistemological essence. We have already elaborated on the infinitude of possible worlds and at this stage we should further consider the relationship between fictional worlds and the actual one. The actual world, while at first sight encompasses large but nonetheless limited number of individuals, is infinite in its potential. Therefore, there is no reason to consider it an incomplete entity: "actual worlds appear to be undoubtly real, complete and consistent, while fictional worlds are intrinsically incomplete and inconsistent" (PAVEL 1986: 74). The actual world is the world of the completeness of our beings and any incompleteness would be incongruous with its status of existence as actual. It is a set of all actual individuals and as such it is complete in its actuality. From an epistemological point of view, we can never be sure that a new piece of evidence or a newly found (scholarly) procedure may appear that would allow the world's inhabitants to fill in the parts considered incomplete at a particular stage of our knowledge and our understanding of the world. Nevertheless, someone might challenge the ontological difference between the actual world and fictional worlds by claiming that even fictional texts might provide the reader with a new piece of information not seen during previous acts of reading and therefore allow him/her to fill in some "kind of incompleteness"; however, this newly constructed fictional world can be "more complete" only in the sense that the reader would be able to understand the fictional piece of information thanks to a new view of the same piece of fictional text, but never in the ontological sense – the text itself "does not move." Thomas Pavel brings new light to this issue by introducing the following terminological difference: "It does not help, some claim, to retort that 'actual' worlds display the same incompleteness; we may well not know whether or not there is life on Mars, but at least in principle the answer exists and waits to be discovered [...] In fiction, indeterminacy strikes at random" (PAVEL 1986: 107).

3. Fictional worlds and the actual world

"Existing in fiction and existing are quite different things" (PARSONS 1999: 50). It is precisely the different foundations of the entities of fictional worlds and the actual one, not to mention their different ontological essences, that demand a detailed and thorough analysis of the specificity and uniqueness of fictional worlds.

Fictional worlds are ad definitio non-actualised possibilities of the same kind and therefore they are ontologically homogenous: "As nonactualized possibles, all fictional entities are of the same ontological nature [...] The principle of ontological homogeneity is a necessary condition for the coexistence, interaction, and communication of fictional persons. It epitomizes the sovereignty of fictional worlds" (DOLEŽEL 1998: 18). In this way, the demarcation line between fictional worlds and the actual one is firmly and unambiguously set: to exist fictionally means to exist through a semiotic medium, whereas actual existence is not mediated by any semiotic channels.

At this point, we should look in more detail at the entity we call the actual world, which is also mediated and created by specific channels – even though a thorough analysis of those concepts which develop from the idea of language constructivism and consider the actual world a cognitive construct given via language in non-fictional channels is not the primary aim of this study. However, a strong restriction on such entities enables us not to consider them as actual worlds: "An object created by a mental process is specified in its features by this very process [...] But a description, verbal or mental, is always incomplete. When we think up an entity, we only specify a subset of its potential properties. It would take a divine mind to run through the list of all possible features and to think up an object into logical completeness" (RYAN 1991: 21). Clearly, both kinds of worlds are accessible through some semiotic channels (texts), which can generate infinite worlds only if they are infinitely descriptive. Ruth Ronen develops this line of thinking by introducing the important concept of *encyclopedia*: "Some theorists of fictionality view the actual world as a stable ontology, some hold that the actual world is a (culturally) variable construct based on ideologically determined encyclopedias" (RONEN 1994: 69). Whereas the former can be termed *actualists* the latter might be termed *discoursists*. Here, we should recall David Lewis' indexical theory (here pg. 15–16) (and also its rejection by the devotees of rigidly logical possible world semantics) and state that some discursive narratologists actually adopted a version of this theory. For example, Marie-Laure Ryan explicitly says that both kinds of worlds are of a discursive essence.

In conclusion, it seems that the only general statement one can make about the relationship between fictional worlds and the actual world is that our knowledge of the actual one can contribute to the reader's conceptualisation of the fictional world – thanks to the accessibility relation defined by Lubomír Doležel: "Fictional Worlds are accessed through semiotic channels" (DOLEŽEL 1998: 20).

3.1 The accessibility relation

Ruth Ronen suggests that the main reason narratologists adopted the concept of possible worlds for the purpose of analysing fictional worlds lies precisely in the fact that the relationship between them was well defined by logical semantics as the "accessibility relation": "Literary theorists and aestheticians make use however of possible worlds because notions of possibility and alternativity enable them to examine the accessibility relations between fictional world and *reality*. That is, literary theorists translate the general notion of accessibility into one particular type of possibility relations between fiction and *reality*" (RONEN 1994: 25). Nevertheless, as much as Ruth Ronen's assertion throws sharp light on the issue of accessibility in the realm of fictional worlds investigation, for a more detailed inquiry of fictional worlds, Brian McHale's definition seems to be of better analytical value: "Given the structure of one possible world, another is said to be accessible to it if by manipulating the first world's entities and their properties one can generate the structure of the world" (McHALE 1987: 35).

For a fictional world to be realised, two important assumptions must be fulfilled: 1) there must exist a material artefact produced by a real writer, a fictional text, which has the potential of generating the specific semantic energy necessary for producing a fictional world; 2) there must exist a real reader who understands the code of the text (narrative) and who, following the text's structure, re-constructs a particular fictional world. Clearly, both the originator and the user of a fictional text are firmly anchored in the actual world. In no case does this statement imply that fictional worlds are mimetic copies of the actual world – the main incongruence lies in the different status of existence of their entities. It has been said above that entities (and structures) of the actual world enter fictional worlds. Nonetheless, it must be emphasised that fictional worlds exist in a different ontological mode than the actual one. Fictional worlds are separated from the actual one (though accessible from it) and non-dependent on it.[22] It can also be assumed that fictional worlds encompass two kinds of objects: domestic (fictional) and immigrant (from the actual world): for example, Terence Parsons distinguishes between "objects *native* to the story versus objects that are *immigrants* to the story" and further stipulates the difference between these kinds of objects: "The distinction is, roughly, whether the story totally 'creates' the object in question, or whether the object is an already familiar one imported into the story" (PARSONS 1980: 51). At the same time, Parsons emphasises that an object exported to a fictional world from the actual one undertakes an ontological transformation and thus become necessarily incomplete (51). Lubomír Doležel exploits this assumption in offering a rigid definition of this transformative process for the purposes of fictional analysis: "Possible-worlds semantics makes us aware that the material coming from the actual world has to undergo a substantial transformation at the world boundary. Because of the ontological sovereignty of fictional worlds, actual-world entities have to be converted into nonactual possibles, with all the ontological, logical, and semantical consequences that this transformation entails" (DOLEŽEL 1998: 21).

From a different point of view, we can agree upon the statement that "facts of the actual world are not constant reference points for the facts of fiction" (RONEN 1994: 12). It does not seem difficult to find examples in support of this statement, especially when we bear in mind that there exist fictional worlds that differ from the actual one, so to speak, at first sight: "fantastic worlds, far removed from, or contradictory to, reality" (DOLEŽEL 1998: 19). Thomas Pavel elaborates on the basic assumption of the different ontological foundations of both types of worlds by introducing the notion of *salient structures* in which "objects belong to two different sets of worlds and have different properties, functions, and ontological weight" (PAVEL 1986: 138). Thus, according to Pavel, fictional worlds are not copies of the actual one, they are even not copies with a different ontological status, but they are subject to specific structures immanent to this particular product of literary semiosis. As Miroslav Červenka emphasises: "in a literary artwork the semantic material from the actual world gains a special function of actualizing the concrete and relevant for the purpose of semiotic systems, which participate in the constitution of the work's world, which is accessible from the actual one but definitely and entirely different from it" (ČERVENKA 2005: 722).

---

22 Ruth Ronen explicitly states that "a fictional world is not a possible world *ramifying* from the actual state of affairs, but a world logically and ontologically *parallel* to the actual world" (RONEN 1994: 91–2).

Červenka also accurately points out the fact that "the difference of a fictional world from the actual world can also lie in an introduction of specific speech acts valid only in the fictional world" (778).

3.2 Fictional and historical counterparts

As noted, some fictional entities (individuals) have their real (or historical) counterparts; nevertheless, the status of these two kinds of entities is essentially different. The notion of a (historical) counterpart is introduced in David Lewis' counterpart theory, which reduces the issue of trans-world-identity to the notion of trans-world resemblance (see here pg. 16). In the realm of counterpart theory, the notion of trans-world resemblance serves to distinguish possible worlds from each other via the minimally different qualities of two different entities belonging to two different possible worlds; however, in the realm of fictional semantics the idea of trans-world resemblance focuses on fictional entities with historical (real, actual) counterparts. The trans-world resemblance concept actually points out a crucial question: how similar can fictional entities and their historical counterparts be and how close can they be? It has been emphasised many times in this study that fictional and actual entities differ essentially. Nevertheless, it is obvious that our knowledge of most historical entities comes to us only via some kind of semantic mediation. This is especially striking when we meet characters in fiction who have historical counterparts of which we have only a very limited knowledge. In this case both individuals are rendered via semiotic systems and therefore seem to be "closer" to each other than the fictional counterparts of two randomly chosen living people. Even so, it must be stated that from an epistemological point of view there is still an essential difference between fictional and historical entities – in spite of the fact that they both arrive via semiotic channels and therefore can be viewed as mere possible counterparts of real people: "The fiction makers practice a radically nonessentialist semantics; they give themselves the freedom to alter even the most typical and well-known properties and life histories of actual (historical) persons when incorporating them in a fictional world. Verisimilitude is a requirement of a certain poetics of fiction, not a universal principle of fiction making. It is essential to the historical Napoleon that he died at Santa Helena. But according to a legend, quoted as a motto of Georg Kaiser's play *Napoleon in New Orleans* (1937), Napoleon was rescued from the island, taken to North America, and died in New Orleans. The nonessentialist semantics of transworld identity applies not only to fictional counterparts of actual persons but equally to the incarnations of a fictional person in different worlds. A fictional person when moved from one world to another might undergo radical alterations" (DOLEŽEL 1998: 17–18).

Ruth Ronen approaches the issue of fictional entities from a different theoretical point of view and emphasises the role of referential theory in the development of fictional semantics. This theory considers proper names as rigid designators and therefore, "A name rigidly refers in contexts that radically diverge from what we know or do not know of the referent in the actual world" (RONEN 1994: 43). Nevertheless, this statement does not influence the relationship between identically named fictional and actual entities. Fictional entities simply do not refer to actual entities, nor do they refer across the ontological border between fictional and actual worlds: "Hamlet, Anna Karenina, Sherlock Holmes, Macbeth's dagger, Des Esseintes' mansion, Proust's *madeleine*, are constantly talked about both by literary critics and by ordinary readers as if these characters and objects were fully individuated and, in some unspecified way, as if they empirically existed. At the same time, names like Anna Karenina and definite descriptions like Proust's *madeleine* do not denote in our world" (PAVEL 1986: 31).

It is obvious that the use of historical individuals in fiction considerably contributes to the final structure of a fictional world. Unfortunately, the only general statement we can articulate with regard to the role of this use is that it contributes to the global structure of the world as a semantic element by bringing specific meaning to it. If we cannot say anything more particular about the entry of historical individuals into fictional worlds, we also cannot say much about individuals referred to by the same name in different fictional worlds. This point of view is strongly supported by Ruth Ronen, who points out two problems caused by connecting fictional and historical counterparts: "(1) it is impossible to demarcate essential properties of Paris which do (or should) recur in each of its literary constructions; (2) diverse descriptive sets can be attributed to the same name in different fictional worlds and therefore descriptions that replace a name in one particular fictional world cannot be transferred or applied to other possible worlds" (RONEN 1994: 127). It seems that we can find an ontological division between the actual world and fictional ones, but consequently between different fictional worlds also, as if, to adapt Thomas Pavel's term, they were salient structures.

3.3 Finitude and completeness

There is a mutual relationship between the finitude and incompleteness of fictional worlds. Their incompleteness is caused by the fact that a fictional text generates a fictional world that is ontologically "poorer" than the actual one.

In a somewhat figurative manner, Umberto Eco proclaims that: "In reality, fictional worlds *are* parasites of the actual world, but they are in effect 'small worlds' which bracket most of our competence of the actual world and allow us to concentrate on a finite, enclosed world, very similar to ours but ontologically poorer" (ECO 1994: 83). Clearly, the claim of ontological "poorerness" can be understood with regard to fictional worlds as a metaphorical representation of the quality of fictional existence. In any case, the incompleteness of worlds of art is accepted both in the general way: worlds of art are not ontologically "comprehensive" (WOLTERSTORRF 1980: 131); as well as in a particular way with regard to fictional characters: "a character created in a piece of fiction is typically incomplete, whereas real people are complete" (PARSONS 1999: 184).

At the very end of this part let me draw a general overview of the most important differences and similarities of all the elaborated types of worlds:

Type of world	Possible world	Fictional world	Actual world
Status of existence	Logical	Fictional	Actual
Infinity of entities	Yes	No	Yes
Completeness	Yes	No	Yes
Number of worlds	Infinite	Infinite	One

4. The structure of fictional worlds

Fictional worlds as entities determined by complex fictional texts are specifically structured. Now, let us try to proceed slightly further in uncovering the specificity of the structure of fictional worlds. Davis Lewis' indexical theory of possible worlds recognises fictional worlds parallel to the actual world, to the extent to which the reader, during the act of reading, actualises (re-constructs) a particular fictional world and considers it the actual one. As much as this way of reasoning can prove itself very useful in terms of a literary pragmatic inquiry, a theoretician must be very careful when working with this concept in order not to fall into a dangerous mimetic trap. One of the strongest supporters of Lewis' indexical theory is Marie-Laure Ryan, who points out the direct similarity between his indexical theory and her own approach to fiction: "the indexical theory of David Lewis's offers a much more accurate explanation of the way we relate to these worlds. Once we become immersed in a fiction, the characters become real for us, and the world they live in momentarily takes the place of the actual world" (RYAN 1991: 21). Ryan continues with a description of the progression of this process: "For the duration of our immersion in a work of fiction, the realm of possibilities is thus recentered around the sphere which the narrator presents as the actual world. As a traveller[23] to this system, the reader of fiction discovers not only a new actual world, but a variety of APWs[24] revolving around it. Just as we manipulate possible worlds through mental operations, so do the inhabitants of fictional universes: their actual world is reflected in their knowledge and beliefs, corrected in their wishes, replaced by a new reality in their dreams and hallucinations" (22).

Ryan's fruitful comparison actually brings us closer not only to a better understanding of the processes we use in order to conceptualise fictional worlds but also closer to their elements and their analysis: "The semantic domain of the text is concatenated by the mental activity of characters. The semantic domain of the text is thus a collection of concatenated or embedded possible worlds" (RYAN 1991: 4). Ruth Ronen comes up with a similar suggestion which seems to be, however, slightly more cautious when speaking about the analogy between fictional and actual worlds: "A fictional world, like any possible world, is analogous to the actual world in that it has its own set of facts and its own subworlds and counter-worlds. As a *world* it contains "an actual world" and a set of possibilities, alternatives, predictions and forecasts non-actualized in the fictional world" (RONEN 1994: 29). Ronen consequently elaborates on her clarification of the interfacing features of both types of worlds: "A fictional world is likewise composed of sets of *entities* (characters, objects, places) and of networks of relations can be described as *organizing principles*: spatial-temporal relations, event and action sequences. Worlds, whether fictional, possible or actual, are hence distinguishable from one another. Yet the fictional world is constructed as a world having its own distinct ontological position, and as a world presenting a self-sufficient system of structures and relations" (8). This declaration successfully fulfils our idea of a structure that can in its totality be viewed as a world. A world which is not a mimetic copy of the actual world, though it is strongly influenced by our concept of the actual world.

Ruth Ronen provides a further elaboration of the structure of fictional worlds. She proclaims a certain part of the world as actualised and places this part at that world's centre. This fictional world's core is, according to Ronen, surrounded by modal satellite worlds: "A fictional universe has its own complex modal structure,

---

23 Not surprisingly, Thomas Pavel uses a similar metaphor in his specific way of reasoning: "We, too, visit fictional lands, inhabit them for a while, intermingle with the heroes" (PAVEL 1986: 85).

24 Actual Personal Worlds.

in which some states are factual and others are hypothetical, or impossible. An analogous modal structure accounts for the relationship between the actualized world of fiction (the factual centre of that world) and other possible worlds of belief, memory, prediction and so on" (RONEN 1994: 41). Now, let us accept Ryan's following idea that "the primary level of conflict is between TAW[25] and one of the worlds of a private domain. Whenever conflict exists objectively in a textual universe, it is found on this level" (RYAN 1991: 120). If so, it is obvious that these modal worlds of characters, worlds of belief, wishes, intentions, etc. are placed outside the part of the world that they co-habit. These worlds are satellites to the co-habited world in a way parallel to that in which individual worlds are satellites of the actual world. This path leads us to an investigation of modal structure and other constraints of fictional worlds, as we will closely examine them in the chapter devoted to intensional function.

4.1 Extensional and intensional structures of fictional worlds

Fictional worlds are complex structures usually consisting of various living and non-living subjects and objects, and the natural laws, relationships and interactions between them. All of a fictional world's entities share the fictional mode of existence given through semiotic media (texts). If we accept the assumption based on the communicative model that a fictional world exists due to the semantic energy generated by a fictional text and is re-constructed by a creative act of reading, a crucial question has to be asked: What is the connection between the structure of a fictional text and the fictional world based on the text; in other words, how is a fictional world's structure determined by the structure of the primary fictional text? For help in answering this question, one should revisit the notions of extension and intension (see here pg. 28–36). The reason is simple: if we are to speak about textual meaning it is important to speak about the two parts of an expression's meaning: about its extensional and intensional meaning.

As has been iterated many times now, under the term extension (of an expression), we understand a set of individuals to which the expression refers in a world; the form of the expression itself is left unexamined. If we speak about the extension of simply composed expressions like "Morning Star" and "Evening Star" (they undoubtly refer to the same object, the planet Venus) they are assigned to the same spatial object and therefore their extensions (extensional meanings) are identical. In terms of more complex expressions like the clauses and sentences of natural language their extensions are, according the principle

---

25 Textual Actual World.

of compositionality, extensions equal to the sum of extensions of particular elements of these expressions. It can easily happen that an extensional transposition of a natural-language sentence is the sentence itself, but generally speaking when seeking an extensional transposition of any natural-language sentence we try to represent the sentence's reality in terms of its important features; usually we use neutral, inexpressive, widely understandable devices in order to deliver the content of the sentence unambiguously. If so, an extensional transposition of the sentence "John is gazing at Luna" will be "John is looking at the Moon" – both sentences express the same extension. An individual called John is performing an action with his eyes and brain and aims the eyes at a spatial object named the Moon; however, their intensions obviously differ. In everyday conversations in natural language we usually use longer communicative units than just one sentence to thoroughly describe the important features of our everyday experience with all the subjectivity and semantic detours needed for emphasising our subjects essential for the experience itself. In this case, a relatively long story about a trip undertaken last week can be extensionally transposed into the sentence: "Yesterday in the morning we took a train from London Waterloo to Windsor, walked along the Thames, then on the Long Walk across the Windsor Park to Egham, had a pint of pale ale at the Red Lion, and returned by train back to London Waterloo." This paraphrase provides us with a relatively neutral expression, which delivers us all the facts important for purely informative purposes. Clearly, we can find more than one paraphrase of our story and the paraphrases will differ in terms of the function and circumstances of transpositions of this sort. When Doležel generally states that "extensional meaning has to be expressed in a metalanguage" (DOLEŽEL 1998: 136), it must be admitted that for the purpose of narration in natural language we can substitute this metalanguage by a paraphrase in natural language. In other words, narration is transposed to a different form of the same language.

In terms of narratives, let us assume that the ultimate framework for the extensional meaning of a fictional narrative is the reality to which the narrative refers: a fictional narrative world, or better, its extensional structure. All the extensional meanings of any novel clearly refer to important semantic features of the fictional world of the novel. Simply put, there is no other framework for such reference. As a parallel, in terms of fictional narratives we also have to define a metalanguage to which we are able to transpose the language of the narrative when seeking its extensional structure: "Every student and reader of literature is familiar with informal extensional representations produced by paraphrasing: themes, content abstracts, story and plot summaries, interpretations" (DOLEŽEL

1998: 136). Necessarily, in the case of fictional narratives that are subsumed to narratives in general, it should be emphasised that there is more than one possible paraphrase of the extensional structure of a fictional world. A complete and unique transposition to extensional meaning would be possible only if we had at our disposal a model for transposing each element of natural language to an extensional meaning. Nevertheless, for the context in which we commonly speak of fictional worlds we usually use a partial transposition-paraphrase, which uncovers the extensional meaning of fictional narratives to the extent required for understanding the narratives. The purpose is very often intertwined with the methodological means we have at our disposal and/or with the intention of our analysis and interpretation of fictional narratives. Telling examples of such paraphrasing fictional narratives are book summaries, which provide us with the extensional structures of particular fictional worlds based on particular fictional texts; strictly speaking, they provide us with structures that are close to the extensional structures, as we will see later. Thanks to these summaries we can gain access to the extensional meaning of a fictional world based on a fictional text that we have never opened and read. Thomas Pavel, in a somewhat psychological comment, connects the extensional structures of fictional worlds with a mental residue at the end of the act of reading of a fictional text. This residue, which can be used as a base for our mental mapping and interpreting the fictional world, is actually the world's extensional structure: "Texts, media, are not just referential paths leading to worlds: to read a text or to look at a painting means already to inhabit their worlds. To argue that we easily forget textual beauties while we remember facts and events derives from a natural propensity to register essential elements and to disregard circumstantial information; but such a propensity does not necessarily entail that we first read texts, then reach the worlds and discard the medium" (PAVEL 1986: 74).[26]

By contrast, intensional meaning is connected with the form of a linguistic representation of an expression: the intensional meanings of the expressions "Morning Star" and "Evening Star" differ: simply whereas the former one refers to the last star in the morning sky, the latter refers to the first star in the evening sky. In a parallel to extensional meaning we can suggest that, in terms of natural

---

26 "The worlds we speak about, actual or fictional, neatly hide their deep fractures, and our language, our texts, appear for a while to be transparent media unproblematically leading to worlds. For, before confronting higher-order perplexities, we explore the realms described by compendia and texts, which stimulate our sense of referential adventure and, in a sense, serve as mere paths of access to worlds: once the goal is reached, the events of the journey may be forgotten" (PAVEL 1986: 73).

language, if intensions of simple expressions differ, consequently the intensions of compound units also differ: natural-langue narratives are definitely compound units of this sort. To keep the same example of the trip to Windsor, we can claim that different people present on the trip would describe the trip itself in different ways using different language means – depending upon whether the person liked the trip, was bored by it, disliked it, and also upon the effect the person wants to have in telling their story to other people (envy, pity, regret). We can hypothesise that the intensional meaning in natural language is expressive and non-neutral because it fully depends on the use of individually chosen linguistic means that the narrator adopts for their relationship to the described reality and the purpose of the narration.

The issue of intensional meaning is very important for the concept of literary narration: intensional meaning in literary narration grows from a complex linguistic structure that is presented by a narrative text and fundamentally structures fictional worlds. Obviously, a narrative text embodies the only platform against which the intensional meaning can be detected and described: "Being fully determined by its texture, intensional meaning is affected by any textual change; it is nonparaphrasable, it slips through the net of "interpretants", it is lost in retelling. Any paraphrasing, any interpretation destroys the intensional meaning in the process of destroying the original texture" (DOLEŽEL 1998: 138). As has been seen, Doležel works in his reasoning from the crucial idea that the principle of compositionality, valid for an extensional meaning, can be applied to the intensional meaning too. If so, it is reasonable to speak of the intensions of narrative texts of which the complexity is the most important quality. Nevertheless, at this point, an essential question has to be raised: how do we grasp intension in a narrative text as an object for further investigation? In the case of extensional meaning we are able to paraphrase the narratives and to investigate the paraphrases; however, we cannot perform the same substitution in terms of the intensional meaning, which is essentially dependent on the form of its expression: every paraphrase thus essentially changes the intension of the compound text. Therefore, the only method available for an intensional investigation of literary texts is, as Doležel strongly claims, to open "the way for us to study intensions *indirectly*, through the observable, analyzable structuring of texture" (DOLEŽEL 1998: 138).

As has just been suggested, when uncovering the intensional meaning we have to investigate the qualities of the fictional text (texture), which, in turn, determines the very structure of the fictional world given by the text: "Ultimately, the formation of the text's intensional meaning is a global, macrostructural happening, just as the organization of its fictional world is" (DOLEŽEL 1998: 139). The final task is thus to uncover the analogies of both structures, respectively, in order to investigate the ways in which the structure of a text—the very basis for the intensional meaning—participates in the structure of a fictional world based on the text.

So far I have discussed extensional and intensional structures of fictional worlds separately. However, at this point it is necessary to emphasise an important epistemological and methodological presumption that already occurs in the extension vs. intensional distinction and fully applies to their respective structures of fictional worlds. As we have seen, extension and intension are inseparable components of a language expression's meaning. Similarly, a narrative text obtains two meaning components, the extensional and the intensional, which both relate to the world generated by the text and participate in the final shape of the world constructed. Therefore, every time we examine fictional worlds' extensional structures separately from their intensional structures we do so purely for analytical reasons.[27] In the real world, these two types of structures are inseparable: "Although extensions and intensions can and must be differentiated in semantic theory, they are by definition complementary in the production of literary meaning" (DOLEŽEL 1998: 142). What is the nature of the relationship between a world's extensional and intensional structures? Doležel explicitly stipulates that: "The fictional worlds [...] are extensional entities. Their constituents, shapes, and structures are not tied to the wording of the constructing fictional text but are fixed by paraphrasing, by a translation of the original texture into extensional representations. But, obviously, fictional worlds are constructed by the author and reconstructed by the reader in and through the fictional text's original wording (texture), that is, as intensional formations" (DOLEŽEL 1998: 139). This can be considered a semiotic answer to the question, but another explanation of the relationship derives from a cognitive perspective: "Our memory seems mostly to register facts and characters, and even when we do remember isolated lines, we usually select gnomic and aphoristic passages, as if an irrepressible referential instinct presses us to go beyond the textual medium" (PAVEL 1986: 73–74).

---

27 Here, let me refer to a similar separation of unseparable entities for methodological purposes: French structuralists, when diferentiating between story and discourse, made a similar move – these two aspects of narration are in fact two sides of the same coin, though investigated separately, each side with a set of specific devices and strategies.

4.2 Narrative modalities

As has become obvious in the course of this study, fictional worlds serve as the basis for creating stories. The category of story has undergone a long development since the 1960s when it was brought to theoretical attention by French structuralists. The modern theory of narrative (or narratology) stemming from the famous structuralist distinction between story and discourse investigates stories in various ways and from various vantage aspects. The 'story-turn' has brought several important insights into the role that stories play in human culture and society, in the arts in general, and in fictional literature in particular. Nevertheless, it is only fictional worlds theory that views stories in the wider realm of their preconditions and milieu.[28] Action theory borrows from the structuralist investigation of stories and sees action as characterised by changes of states of affairs. According to action theory, articulated especially in the work of George von Wright, actions are subject to formative operations shaping narrative worlds. Doležel elaborates on von Wright's suggestions and develops a system of four modalities which, together with their respective constraints, actually shape fictional worlds in order to produce stories. The system combines *alethic, deontic, axiological* and *epistemic* operators with the quantifiers some, none and all, resulting in four groups of triplets: possible, impossible, necessary for alethic operators; permitted, prohibited, obligatory for deontic operators; good, bad, indifferent for axiological operators; and finally known, unknown, and believed for epistemic ones (see DOLEŽEL 1998: 114). All of these operators can be considered either in relation to one particular subject of a possible world (subjective modalities) or in relation to the world itself (codexal modalities). Ryan connects Doležel's system of operators with the notion of conflict: "Conflict is not simply the complication or thickening of the plot that occurs between exposition and resolution, but a more or less permanent condition of narrative universes [...] Plots originate in knots – and knots are created when the lines circumscribing the worlds of the narrative universe, instead of coinciding, intersect with each other. In order to disentangle the lines in their domain, characters resort to plotting, with the almost inevitable effect of creating new knots in some other

---

28 The connection between stories and worlds has been examined extensively. Among others, David Herman in his book *Story Logic: Problems and Possibilities of Narrative* (2002) provides us with a key concept of *storyworld* and its detailed analysis. However, as Jiří Koten states: "the differences between theoretical conceptions of fictional worlds and story worlds steming from the origin of their interdisciplinary borrowings as well as their very delimations and possible utilizations" (KOTEN 2011: 52).

domain" (RYAN 1991: 120). By defining the universes for creating stories and the operators that control the production of stories, Doležel not only contributes to the tradition of so-called narrative grammars, but also takes the tradition a step further: whereas narrative grammars are descriptive systems that provide us with descriptions of possible narrative constellations—that of stories—Doležel gives us a system that accommodates the general preconditions of story-making: Narrative modalities as formative operations that shape "narrative worlds into orders that have the potential to produce (generate) stories. Modalities are the main formative operations of this kind" (DOLEŽEL 1998: 113).

4.3 Intensional functions

Intensional functions formally display the analogy between the texture's structure and the intensional structure of a fictional world. Doležel defines these functions with regard to the general definition of intension as functions operating "from the fictional text's texture to the fictional world" (DOLEŽEL 1998: 139). Intensional functions transmit the structure of a texture to that of a fictional world: it is a "global regularity of texture that affects the structuring of the fictional world" (139). The path to an analysis of fictional functions starts with a fictional text in the structure of which these functions are anchored. The first step towards their examination is to detect and describe global regularities of the fictional text's texture; the second step is to analyse the ways in which intensional functions participate in a fictional world's structure. Intensional functions obviously play an important role in the author's construction of a fictional world as well as in the reader's reconstruction of it; therefore, they seem to be good means of entering into fictional worlds.

In his *Heterocosmica* (1998), Doležel thoroughly analyses and describes two intensional functions which, according to him, substantially participate in fictional worlds structure, namely the *authentication intensional function* which generally distributes "existence" within a fictional world; and the *saturation intensional function* which, with the same generality, distributes the "density" of the given world.

4.4 Authentication function

The authentication intensional function is inseparably connected with the specific status of the existence of fictional worlds and their entities that are based on a particular fictional text: "The text's power to grant fictional existence is explained by the procedure of authentication and formally expressed in the intensional function of authentication" (DOLEŽEL 1998: 145). Doležel, when positing the authentication intensional function, argues that this investigation proceeds in two closely related steps: first, it is necessary to analyse the ways in which this function is founded in a text, that is, which regularities of texture this function is anchored in; second, one must investigate the relationship between the regularity of its occurrence and fictional existence, which is to say, define the range of the function.

As has been claimed, fictional worlds are the ultimate referential frameworks of fictional texts. All the text's parts refer to a particular fictional world that exists through the medium of the fictional text: "Possible worlds semantics hence does not deal with the denotative value of expressions in the actual world, but with the ways in which denotations are determined in a possible world" (RONEN 1994: 28).

While Doležel developed the notion of intensional functions, some initial suggestion concerning the ideas of intensional functions derive already from the work of Pavel, who in his *Fictional Worlds* (1986) makes the first step in an authentication intensional function analysis and introduces the notion of fictional states of affairs: "the worlds of fiction come in various sizes, all adequately represented by texts and well perceived by the penetrating eye of the reader or spectator. Under this assumption, the size of a fictional world is directly related to textual size: the fictional states of affairs are those described or easily inferred from the sentences of the text" (PAVEL 1986: 96). Nevertheless, Pavel's demand for *description* and *inference* seems to be very general for the purposes of a detailed analysis of the phenomena under investigation. Therefore, Doležel takes a step further and, in analogy to J. L. Austin's notion of a performative speech act, considers the power of fictional texts to create fictional worlds, i.e., their authentication power, to be "a special kind of performative force" (DOLEŽEL 1998: 146). J. L. Austin's performative speech act, when uttered under felicitous conditions, is one where "the uttering of the sentence is, or is a part of, the doing of an action" (AUSTIN 1971: 5). Analogically, for utterances of a fictional text Doležel stipulates: "If uttered felicitously, the literary performative changes a possible entity into a fictional fact. In other words, fictional fact is a possible entity authenticated by a felicitous literary speech act" (DOLEŽEL 1998: 146). By introducing the crucial term of a *fictional fact*, Doležel actually gains an important means to get to the very base of fictional existence – a fictional fact exists when successfully[29] "uttered" by a fictional

---

29 Clearly, Doležel's demand for a *successful utterance* belongs to the realm of literary pragmatics.

text. This term actually connects the semantics of an utterance with fictional semantics.

Doležel undertakes an analysis of all possible preconditions of (fictional) success and comes to the conclusion that, in narratives, not just one type of utterance exists – on the contrary, narratives are heterogeneous with regard to utterances. If the authentication intensional function is defined as a function from texture to fictional existence, then "the illocutionary diversity of literary texts means a diversity of authentication 'authorities'" (DOLEŽEL 1998: 147). Thus, the linguistic features of particular utterances directly influence the degree of fictional existence of particular fictional entities. This direct dependence of the degree of fictional existence of fictional facts on the structure of fictional utterances implies that this specific kind of existence is an intensional phenomenon: "The claim that fictional existence is an intensional phenomenon has radical consequences for fictional semantics. It means that fictional existence is not confined to the polarity of actual existence ("to be or not to be"). *To exist fictionally means to exist in different modes, ranks, and degrees*" (147).

The essential dichotomy of utterances in narrative texts is firmly connected with their "source." In narratives we can find two sources for narrative utterances: a) the narrator, and b) fictional individuals. According to Doležel: "The opposition creates a tension within the narrative text that ultimately gave rise to a gamut of narrative discourse types, ranging from a strictly objective to a purely subjective" (DOLEŽEL 1998: 147). One important question remains: How do these two sources of narrative utterances influence a fictional world's structure? In other words, how is the fictional world's structure influenced by the narrator's or a character's utterances and which degrees of fictional existence gain these utterances? Doležel estimates that "entities introduced in the discourse of the anonymous third-person narrator are *eo ipso* authenticated as fictional facts, while those introduced in the discourse of the fictional persons are not" (149).[30]

---

30 It seems that Felix Martínez-Bonati, when speaking about true statements, reasons in a similar manner: "For the fundamental understanding of all narration, the requirement is that the mimetic sentences of the narrator, but not those of the characters, be accepted as true. If a conflict arises (contradiction, opposition, discrepancy) between the *singular* statements (i.e. statements concerning individuals) of the narrator and those of a character, the character is *at once* understood to be.– intentionally or unintentionally – in error (MARTÍNEZ-BONATI 1981: 31)." However, it is important to see that the similarity between the two conceptions is not deeply founded – Martínez-Bonati's singular statements are restricted to one narrative level, and thus they do not solve the problem of authentication at a general level.

As evidence of this statement he uses Quixote's fight with windmills as it is rendered in Cervantes' novel *Don Quixote*: whereas windmills are constituted by the third-person narrator, the giants are introduced by the speech act of the first person-narrator, Don Quixote; therefore, the windmills are authenticated eio ipso, whereas the giants are not.

Doležel generalises this rule and distinguishes two domains of fictional worlds with regard to the source of fictional statements: "Fictional facts constructed by authoritative narrative constitute the factual domain, the nonauthenticated possibles introduced in the character's discourse – the virtual domain of the fictional world" (DOLEŽEL 1998: 150).[31] Ruth Ronen only confirms such a division of fictional worlds when separating factual and non-factual elements of fictional worlds: "Most literary worlds contain a core of fictional facts but also nonfactual elements like the beliefs, desires or predictions of a character or narrator, elements that do not *obtain* in the fictional world" (RONEN 1994: 31).

Certainly, it is challenging to focus on narratives that do not provide the narration of an authoritative narrator at all. Even in these narratives fictional entities and events can become fictional facts and, in turn, fictional worlds consisting of these fictional facts are paraphrasable – in other worlds, these fictional worlds have their extensional structures consisting of fictional facts. Doležel admits that "fictional persons possess some degree of authentication authority […] but we must add immediately that this authority depends on strict conditions, three of which seem to be necessary: first, the speaker has to be trustworthy ("reliable"); second, there has to be consensus among the persons of the world with respect to the entity in question; third, the virtual must never be disauthenticated in the authoritative narrative. If these conditions are met, the virtual becomes a fictional fact" (DOLEŽEL 1998: 150). These conditions seem to be rigid enough to guarantee fictional entities the possibility of becoming fictional facts equal to those authenticated by authorial narrators. Thus, the factual domain of a fictional world encompasses entities authenticated either by the direct authentication power of the narrator or by a procedure authenticating the fictional character's statements: "As to the virtual domain, the domain of possibles that remain

---

31 Ruth Ronen actually refers to the description of procedures, preconditions, and degrees of authorisation: "only some fictional propositions come from an authorial source, whereas others come from a source to whom the power of narration has been delegated with different degrees of authorization (as demonstrated by the difference between an omniscient narrator, a person narrating about his younger self in the first person, and an unreliable narrator" (RONEN 1994: 92). Unfortunately, the author does not provide a more detailed elaboration of this issue.

nonauthentic, it divides into private domains, the beliefs, visions, illusions, and errors of individual fictional persons" (151). Surely, Don Quixote's belief that he is bravely fighting real enemies belongs to this case.

It seems to be obvious that the division between the factual and virtual domains of a fictional world strongly determines the world's basic stratification: "Variations of authority produce a fictional world whose structure is fundamentally modal, containing sets of fictional facts alongside sets of relativized elements attributed to characters' knowledge, beliefs, thoughts, predictions. The interaction of speakers with propositions produces a world hierarchically organized where facts, quasi-facts and nonfacts constitute the totality of the world" (RONEN 1994: 176). What then is the world's stratification? Is it possible to describe this stratification? To answer these questions most theoreticians usually employ an analogy between the actual world and the worlds of its inhabitants: the central part is the world's core ($\approx$ the actual world shared by all characters), which is surrounded by satellite worlds ($\approx$ individual worlds, fictional character's worlds, their belief, faith, conviction...).[32] Ruth Ronen further connects this model with the status of particular fictional entities: "Constructed as a parallel world, every fictional world includes a core of facts around which orbit sets of states of affairs of diminishing fictional actuality" (8–9). From a purely terminological point of view it should be added that, for example, Pavel names the world of fictional facts, placing it at the core of a fictional world as a "primary world": "Every world encompasses a primary narrative world, the world of fictional facts" (PAVEL 1986: 567).

4.4.1 The principle of minimal departure

Marie-Laure Ryan introduces the concept of the minimal departure principle in order to describe the way in which the reader fills in the gaps in his reconstruction of a fictional world. Ryan describes the parameters of what she understands the concept of a minimal departure principle to encompass: "This law – to which I shall refer as the principle of minimal departure – states that we reconstrue the central world of a textual universe in the same way we reconstrue the alternate possible worlds of nonfactual statements: as conforming as far as possible to our

---

32 Martínez-Bonati explicitly refers to the similarity between fictional and actual characters: "The speech of the characters that remains ordinary speech and does not become narration has no more claim to credibility than that of speakers in the real world" (MARTÍNEZ-BONATI 1981: 31).

representation of AW.[33] We will project upon these worlds everything we know about reality, and we will make only the adjustments dictated by the text" (RYAN 1991: 51). Ryan continues with the claim that: "The point of the text is to call to mind the principle of minimal departure – only to block its operation" (58). Nevertheless, it seems difficult to accept the fact that a text merely blocks the reader's mimetic procedures. If this were the case, there is no guarantee that this knowledge of reality would encompass only cognitive procedures and leave the non-cognitive ones aside. The actual world experienced by an individual differs from the actual world, which is a set of our knowledge of reality, a cultural construct. It seems that readers during their reconstruction of fictional worlds employ not only the actual world/cultural construct, but also the world of their everyday, non-rationalised experience. In a way, Ryan actually supports this idea by suggesting that "It is by virtue of the principle of minimal departure that readers are able to form reasonably comprehensive representations of the foreign worlds created through discourse, even though the verbal representation of these worlds is always incomplete" (RYAN 1991: 52). However, I myself cannot see one single reason why fictional worlds reconstructed by the reader should be complete in this sense. On the contrary, the quality of completeness fits with their ontological background. Terence Parsons supports this view when he explicitly distinguishes between empirically and semantically obtained experiences, by raising a general question that he subsequently answers: "Is it that we add known empirical generalizations to what is stated in the text, and make obvious inferences from the combination? Certainly not, for often a text contradicts known facts" (PARSONS 1999: 178). It also seems that Pavel is considerably more cautious than Ryan when negotiating the issue of the reader's reconstruction of a fictional world: "This convention [of fiction] regulates the behavior of the readers by requiring from them a maximal participation oriented toward the optimal exploitation of textual recourses" (PAVEL 1986: 123). Pavel here not only points out the difference between the perception of fictional and actual worlds, but also emphasises the semantic independence and self-sufficiency of fictional discourse.[34]

---

33 The Actual World.

34 Marie-Laure Ryan's mimetic position can be detected in her other suggestion that: "The gaps in the representation of the textual universe are regarded as withdrawn information, and not as ontological deficiences of this universe itself" (RYAN 1991: 53).

4.5 Saturation function

Fictional worlds, as stipulated, are incomplete due to the finitude of fictional texts that accommodate them. Doležel, when defining the intensional saturation function, bases his concept of the function on the relationship between the incompleteness of a fictional text (its finitude) and the saturation of a fictional world: "we should recognize that the fictional text's texture manipulates incompleteness in many different ways and degrees, determining the world's saturation" (DOLEŽEL 1998: 169). Pavel also refers to this incompleteness and considers gaps (the results of this incompleteness) an important element in modern fiction: "The radical gap is but one of numerous devices modern and postmodern texts display in their eagerness to lay bare the properties of fiction" (PAVEL 1986: 108). Gaps are immanent with regard to fictional worlds and due to their very essence it is impossible to find a procedure that would enable us to distinguish them from fictional worlds: "Between logically necessary analytic implications, the inferences of interpreting critics and readers, and the fantasies of the reader, who identifies himself with the main hero and covers the hero with pictures of his own youth – between these different possibilities and degrees of filling in the incompleteness of a fictional world according to the actual world yawn undefined gaps" (ČERVENKA 2003: 30).

According to Doležel, who has undertaken the most detailed analysis of intensional functions, a fictional fact is a part of the determinate domain of a fictional world and is sufficiently authenticated by the authentication function. In brief, fictional facts set the factual domain of a fictional world. Another domain of the fictional world is the virtual one; the third and final possibility is that of a gap in the fictional world: "If no texture is written (zero texture), a gap arises in the fictional-world structure. Gaps, let us repeat, are a necessary and universal feature of fictional worlds. Yet particular fictional texts vary the number, the extent, and the functions of the gaps by varying the distribution of zero texture" (DOLEŽEL 1998: 169–170). Nevertheless, it should be said that the division of a fictional world into factual and virtual domains on the one hand and gaps on the other results in a relatively coarse distinction; therefore, Doležel turns his attention to the implicitness of texts and their ability to produce implicit meanings: "Today we know that implicitness is a universal feature of texts," and points out the exclusive position of fictional texts: "in literary texts, implicitness is cultivated, it is a factor of their aesthetic effectiveness" (172–173). Two questions remain: how is the implicit meaning based in a fictional text? And how can the implicit meanings be uncovered? Doležel, in order to answer these questions, actually starts from the point that the agents of implicit meaning in texts are "both negative (lacunae) and positive (hints)" (174). Clearly, both of these elements are based in the text's texture, which is their only source. The procedures which serve for uncovering these implicit meanings do not, according to Pavel, substantially differ from the cognitive procedures commonly used in the actual world: "Therefore travel to fictional lands does not necessarily entail a weakening of the usual methods of inference, common-sense knowledge, and habitual emotions" (PAVEL 1986: 88).

In order to shed light on the implicit meaning of a literary text, Doležel adopts the notion of *inference*, which represents a cognitive procedure wider than the logical concept of implication:[35] "For the semantics of fictional narrative, inferences regarding aspects and constituents of acting are of special significance" (DOLEŽEL 1998: 175). Nevertheless, it seems that inferences of plot elements are not the only inferences functioning in fictional texts: "the typical process during the constitution of a fictional world is estimating the character of the heroes based on their deeds" (ČERVENKA 2003: 30).

The so-called existential presupposition can be easily supported by numerous forms of evidence. When, for example, in the above quoted beginning of Franz Kafka's *Metamorphosis* the reader realises that a character called Gregor Samsa woke up in his bed from anxious dreams and discovers that he has turned into a kind of insect, the existential presupposition teaches us that Gregor Samsa exists, so does his bed – regardless of the type of existence they possess.

It is obvious that this procedure "itself provides us only with trivial implied meanings, reformulations of the explicit texture" (DOLEŽEL 1998: 176). The implicit meaning is a structured meaning and, by presupposition, the inferred existence of a fictional world's entities clearly belongs only to a basic level of the implicit meaning: "Cognitive operations have to be activated in order to recover more than trivial or self-evident implied meanings" (176). Clearly, these operations are not restricted to the realm of fiction: they play important roles in human communication in general and enable the participants to create several encyclopedias that serve as bases for communication. Simply speaking, encyclopedias are storehouses for information: "Encyclopedia as shared communal knowledge varies with cultures, social groups, historical epochs, and for this reason relativizes the recovery of implicit meaning" (177). Obviously, here we refer to the actual world encyclopedia, which is the storehouse of our knowledge about the actual world. However, we have to keep in mind that this knowledge has already undergone the process of semantisation: "The actual world is the one

---

35 Presupposition can be defined as follows: A is a presupposition of A' if A implicates A' and at the same time the negation of A ($\neg$A) also implies A'.

we know through a multitude of world pictures or stated descriptions, and these pictures are epistemic worlds that are frequently mutually exclusive. The whole of the picture of the actual world is the potentially maximal and complete encyclopedia of it (on the purely regulative nature of such a potential encyclopedia)" (ECO 1990: 67). Every individual keeps their private individual encyclopedia within the realm of the general one and these individual encyclopedias overlap. An individual encyclopedia is a structured system combining several levels of information. The individual encyclopedias differ from each other and they can also differ from the generally accepted actual world encyclopedia.

4.5.1 Fictional encyclopedia

Doležel explicitly expresses his idea of a fictional encyclopedia as follows: "Knowledge about a possible world constructed by a fictional text constitutes a fictional encyclopedia. Fictional encyclopedias are many and diverse, but all of them to a greater or lesser degree digress from the actual-world encyclopedia" (DOLEŽEL 1998: 177). In relation to this point, Pavel undertakes a highly interesting move towards game theory when explaining the widening of the reader's encyclopedia: "while a naive reader knows these and only these [basic] rules, more advanced strategies can gradually become available through training and practice" (PAVEL 1986: 126).

Necessarily, different fictional encyclopedias belonging to different fictional worlds vary according to their "distance" from the actual world. When uncovering the implicit meanings of a realist novel the reader can rely on the actual world's encyclopedia – sometimes with minor corrections, simply because realist worlds are usually set in certain milieus, close to the actual time. Nevertheless, when reading narratives where fictional worlds are seriously detached from the actual one, for example, due to the existence of different natural laws, completely new objects and relationships – the actual world's encyclopedia is not fully sufficient: "In other words, knowledge of the fictional encyclopedia is absolutely necessary for the reader to comprehend a fictional world. The actual-world encyclopedia might be useful, but it is by no means universally sufficient" (DOLEŽEL 1998: 181). It should be mentioned at this point that the actual world's encyclopedia is never fully sufficient for uncovering a fictional world, but always somehow stays in the background of the fictional encyclopedia. Since Umberto Eco called fictional worlds "parasites" of the actual one (here pg. 48) we consequently can view the fictional encyclopedia as a parasite on the actual encyclopedia – to an extent they overlap and to an extent they differ. Let us take Pegasus as an example of a purely fictional individual. Pegasus is an inhabitant of the world of ancient mythology and we are convinced that it does not exist in the actual world. Nevertheless, even in the fictional encyclopedia, Pegasus is a winged horse[36] and therefore, this individual combines two qualities: "to be a horse" and "to have wings," which both have meaning in the actual world encyclopedia. From its very origin, Pegasus is a part of a fictional encyclopedia and is publicly perceived in this way. Nonetheless, as an entity Pegasus has also enriched our actual world encyclopedia even though it does not exist in the actual world – only as a part of our cultural mythology.

4.6 Fictional and historical worlds

In this section, which can be considered an appendix to the main body of the fictional world theory, I would like to draw our attention to a specific application of the fictional world theory to one of the most crucial issues of contemporary literary theoretical investigation: the notion of fiction and fictionality. Literary theoreticians have been seeking the essence of literariness for a long period of time. In the modern history of literary theoretical inquiry, I would emphasise Roman Jakobson, Käte Hamburger, Barbara Hernstein Smith, John Searle, and Roland Barthes among other scholars who have tried to demarcate the realm of literature. It seems quite fair to say here that the majority of these attempts do differentiate fiction from non-fiction. Such attempts are based on a description of the uniqueness of fictional discourse. Nevertheless, fictional world theory offers, as we will see shortly, a specific means that enables Lubomír Doležel to contribute substantially to the present debate in his most recent book, *Possible Worlds of Fiction and History: The Postmodern Stage* (2010). As much as fictional worlds are obviously discursive entities (and a lot of attention in this study has been paid to this fact), Doležel mainly focuses on fictional and historical worlds as macrostructural entities. In his approach he compares:

a)   the ways in which fictional and historical worlds function: "Fictional worlds are imaginary alternates of the actual world; historical worlds are cognitive models of the actual past" (DOLEŽEL 2010: 33);

b)   the ways in which they are structured: "In mythology, supernatural beings (deities, demons, spirits, and so on) are an integral part of the constellation of fictional persons and make their actional contribution to the story. In

---

36 A strictly realist logician would question whether this individual is still a horse – when winged, respectively whether this individual has a reference. Obviously, this objection does not matter to us – for us Peagasus is a winged horse and exists fictionally.

historical worlds events cannot be assigned to divine agency (even if the historian is a believer). Historical worlds are worlds of natural agents" (35);

c)	the constellations of their actors: if new evidence shows the presence (absence) of an agent in a historical world it is necessary to add (remove) this agent to (from) the world; "No such restriction applies to the constellation of agents in a fictional world" (36); and

d)	their incompleteness: both types of worlds are incomplete; however, "the character, distribution, and treatment of gaps in fiction differ fundamentally from those of history" (37).

It should be said that Doležel, following these four criteria, delivers a consistent and convincing model of the differences in the ontological and epistemological qualities of the two kinds of worlds. At the same time, the author actually offers more than a systematic model, displaying the differences of several aspects of fictional and historical worlds. By doing so he simply confirms that the language-constructivist precondition connected with the post-structuralist philosophy of language, which omits the difference between in-language-based worlds, is invalid.

Nevertheless, Doležel does not stop here and proceeds further by focusing on postmodern fictional and historical worlds, which represent the ultimate challenge with regard to differentiation between fictional and historical worlds due to the fact that many postmodern historians seem reluctant to differentiate between the production of fictional and historical narratives. The worlds founded on these narratives can be compared only by a detailed analysis of the worlds produced by fictional and historical postmodern texts. Therefore, Doležel undertakes such an analysis of the epistemological and ontological qualities of several postmodern fictional and historical worlds by the postmodern historian Simon Schama. He comes to the conclusion that, in spite of the fact that postmodern fictional and historical worlds are strikingly similar, Schama engages "both historical research techniques and fictional imagination, to construct both historical and fictional worlds without confusing them" (DOLEŽEL 2010: 83). As can be seen, Doležel's view of the difference between postmodern fictional and historical worlds is determined by the ways in which they are constructed: free imagination vs. evidence-based research.

III. Literary transduction

1. General specification

The notion of literary transduction stems from a specific approach to literary artworks, one inspired by the theory of information. In this respect a literary artwork is considered a means of communication between its sender and receiver, as a carrier of specific information. This approach lies at the very heart of modern thinking about literature and has inspired various currents of literary theoretical investigation. The general scheme of the communicative model is source ? codification ? transmissional channel ? encoding ? receiver, and in the case of a literary transmission, transforms into sender (author) ? message ? receiver (reader). This model has become a widely accepted for the existence and functioning of literary artworks. From a semantic point of view, the most challenging category is represented by "message" or "communication" with all its levels and specific structures: "The theory of information opens extensive possibilities for employing exact methods in literary theoretical practice due to the fact that within this theory exact procedures are used for an analysis of a message and its transmission; literary artworks are basically messages" (LEVÝ 1971: 11).

At the general level of communication we face some inconvenience. The first is the direction of the communication. The one-way communication model as applied to literary communication brings with it a certain asymmetry. Not only from a temporal point of view (in that the act of writing precedes the act of reading), but also with regard to the flow of semantic energy, which is crucial for the construction and re-construction of a fictional world. Nevertheless, this one-way model is connected with another issue, which is the message as a source of semantic energy itself.

A literary artwork is based on a creative activity of which the result is a literary text. The text is consequently the necessary precondition of a receptive activity: "Theory of information does not view a literary artwork as a static system of which inner relations can be observed from various perspectives but as an in-time realized structure of elements which is the result of selective and combinatory activities of the author and which also carries information which the receiver encodes, with minor changes caused by the differences between the codes of the author and the receiver" (LEVÝ 1971: 14). This suggestion leads us to the very essence of literary communication. As has been already stated, in the communicative model scheme the transmission of literary information is asymmetrical. This asymmetry is firmly connected with the notion of code.

Obviously, the reader must share the code with the writer in order to be able to communicate via the text at all. However, there are several levels of the code that can be shared by both subjects of communication; there are also levels that are not always shared absolutely due to the possible distance (spatial, temporal, and cultural) of the subjects. In any case, there is always a fictional world constructed at the end of an act of reading. Certainly, there appears a need to find out one criterion (or a set of criteria) to help us decide whether the reader's reconstruction of a fictional world is "successful." The extensional structure of a fictional world seems the right path to search for this criterion. Thus we can formulate the (very general) criterion as follows: all paraphrases articulated by the readers about a fictional world based on a particular fictional text should overlap in those features that are crucial for the overall structure of the world.

Obviously, the readers' concretisations should correspond not only in their determined domains, but also in their sub-determined domains, since the domains are defined by fictional worlds theory (here pg. 62). In both cases, this is a matter of correspondence of those elements that are crucial for a fictional world's construction; the lack of these elements could cause plot-, character- and context-ruptures, which would ruin the possibility of its complex perspective. In other words, the reader, during their reconstruction of a fictional world, should not 'lose' any important entity inhabiting the world or omit any important relationship that might contribute to the successful paraphrase of the world. This presumption clearly applies to both explicit and implicit meanings.

The next question is: is this knowledge of the code of literary communication a sufficient condition for understanding a literary work? Probably not, simply due to the fact that we intuitively understand that "the difficulty of drawing a line does not obscure the palpable difference between understanding the language of a poem, in the sense that one could provide a rough translation into another language, and understanding the poem" (CULLER 1975: 114). A work's meaning is a complex structured whole with complicated relationships between its levels. According to fictional worlds theory, a literary artwork's meaning can be identified with a fictional world. This claim actually opens the way to an analysis of its meaning: if a literary artwork's meaning is understood as a fictional world, it can then be analysed by analysing that world's structure.

Both elements of narrative meaning, the explicit and the implicit, participate in a fictional world's construction. In terms of explicit meanings, the reader's knowledge of the code of communication should be sufficient for the reader to enter them; the implicit ones are founded in a more complex manner. In order to come to terms with these, the textual instruction has to meet the reader's activity:

"However right they may be, the value judgments of the reader are caused by some stimulus within the text" (RIFFATERRE 1959: 162). The precondition of a successful application of this procedure is the *reader's competence*, which is a term introduced by Jonathan Culler: "Anyone lacking this knowledge, anyone wholly unacquainted with literature and unfamiliar with the conventions by which fictions are read, would, for example, be quite baffled if presented with a poem. His knowledge of the language would enable him to understand phrases and sentences but he would not know, quite literally, what to *make* of this strange concatenation of phrases. He would be unable to read it *as* literature – as we say with emphasis to those who would use literary works for other purposes – because he lacks the complex 'literary competence' which enables others to proceed" (CULLER 1975: 114). The reader's competence defined in this way is a necessary condition of a "successful" reading: it cultivates and limits. The main preconditions of such competence are the above mentioned fictional and actual worlds' encyclopedias.

Ultimately, the encyclopedias enable us to "enter" fictional worlds – structures with high semantic potentials. These encyclopedias are actualised by every act of reading. Furthermore, individual concretisations overlap in ways that make certain aspects of them invariant. Needless to say, these concretisations are strictly governed by the regulatives of fictional texts and therefore differ from the term concretisations introduced by Roman Ingarden in *Das Literarische Kunstwerk* (1931). For fictional worlds semantics it is absolutely unacceptable that the readers fill in the fictional worlds' gaps during their acts of reading: gaps cannot be filled and actually are not supposed to be filled. According to Doležel, with regard to fictional narratives, we lack the procedures with which to fill the gaps – gaps are an inevitable and meaningful part of the structure of fictional worlds.[37]

If a literary artwork is understood to be a communicative means between writer and reader and if the purpose of this communication is a transfer of specific information that founds a fictional world, it is important to focus on the issue of intentionality. Intentionality as regards the reader is undoubtedly present in every act of reading. As Jonathan Culler states: "Reading is not an innocent activity" (CULLER 1975: 129). Similarly, no one can really question the author's intention to encode a fictional world within a fictional text during his/her act of writing. How can we explain then that particular readers' concretisations of the same

---

37 Unlike the case of historical narratives, in terms of fictional narratives, we lack procedures that would enable us to fill in gaps in fictional worlds due to the fact that there is nothing that could be inserted into the gaps, no witness, no evidence, and no new discovery. Gaps are just an inevitable part of a fictional-world structure.

fictional texts often differ from each other? This can be clearly seen when comparing readers' paraphrases of the text. Let us assume that an author develops a particular fictional world in his/her mind prior to the act of writing. He/she uses (natural) language as a code for encoding this world into a text. These procedures actually result in two restrictions. First, the mental image of the fictional world is restricted by the code – or (natural) language – used in order to encode the world, which is as close to the original shape as possible. Second, the encoded world is necessarily incomplete due to the finitude of the fictional texts. These two restrictions are, to a great extent, responsible for the existence of the above mentioned invariant present in the readers' concretisations. The first restriction is connected to extensional meanings: the meaning cannot be interpreted by the readers in ways that would essentially differ from meanings understood by the writer – due to the code shared. The interpretation of implicit meanings has much to do with the readers' competence and also with the procedures they use in their everyday communication in order to uncover implicit meanings in a language. It is obvious that, due to the subjective essence of these procedures and competences, the final shapes of fictional worlds differ according to the interpreting subject-reader. In brief, some of the intensional meanings are uncovered, while some stay uncovered. In addition, the finitude of fictional texts enables the receivers of the texts to accommodate fictional worlds with entities not explicitly or implicitly postulated by fictional texts.

In the 1960s the theory of information developed a theoretical system for the transmission of information based on terms; such as, the value of information, redundancy, and entropy. Basic axioms connected with these notions can be used for literary theoretical investigation. One of the most important axioms says that the amount of information conveyed by a set of signs is in direct proportion to the probability that a particular sign appears in a certain sequence.[38] This axiom potentially provides research into literary syntax with a new source of inspiration. If literary artworks are understood as specific information, the above terms can also be applied to the specific transmission of this information between the writer and the reader. Generally, the value of information is related to the probability of the occurrence of an element after a succession of other elements. When applied to the level of a literary artwork this definition implies that the highest value of information can be found at those places with the occurrence of the

---

38 The amount of information is defined as $I = \log P1/P0$, where P1 is the probability of an event after receiving the information and P0 is the probability of the event before receiving the information.

least expected elements. Nevertheless, at this point, it should be emphasised that literary artworks must contain a certain amount of redundant information in order for them to be viewed and perceived as literary artworks, and also in order to be interpreted as a representation of a genre, trend, or period of literary development. This redundancy can be found at several structural levels: story, plot, composition, and style. Redundancy in literary artworks decreases the value of information but at the same time it is a necessary precondition of the works. Moreover, the term redundancy is firmly linked to Umberto Eco's term of the model reader: the redundancy "shows" the reader the paths to take on their walks in the fictional woods. This redundancy, of course, also serves as a very important element in the process of the formation of the readers' encyclopedias.

2. Intertextuality

The notion of intertextuality, especially after having undertaken a rapid development in literary theoretical and cultural contexts of twentieth century thought, is rather complex. Complexity, as I intend it here, does not refer to some form of inadequate or unsystematic investigation or its results. Rather, I use the term here to "characterize something with many parts in intricate arrangement," to rephrase its commonly accepted definition. In relation to intertextuality, the term complexity can be understood as a set of views and strategies that have surrounded (literary) texts and their connections as the central point of their investigation; indeed, it is impossible to provide a scholarly analysis of a literary text without referring to the connections between particular literary works, genres, periods, and tendencies. The notion of intertextuality in literary theoretical investigation can serve as a means for the investigation of a wide scale of conceivable relationships between literary artworks – from purely textual links between particular artworks to a network of connections between broad sets of them. The re-thinking of older ideas and setting of new ones during the golden age of (French) structuralist and post-structuralist thought served especially to make intertextuality a term that encompasses the whole process of literary communication. Starting from Bakhtin, who stated that "the word in language is half someone else's" (BAKHTIN 1984: 294) in support of his idea of semantic relativism, the idea of intertextuality is used to describe various aspects of literary communication and has become a part of pragmatic and sociological approaches to literature. This attitude is especially prominent in Julia Kristeva's claims that to study a text from an intertextual point of view means to study it "as such within (the text of) society and history" (KRISTEVA 1980: 37), these things actually being products of a text-production activity themselves. The danger of this attitude when taken as a basis for the serious research of intertextuality is obvious and pointed out by Roland Barthes in his skepticism towards the "traceability" of the connections between texts. Indeed, it would be possible to stop here and proclaim, for example, that all genre investigation and a vast portion of literary comparative investigation are based on a purely optional set of preconditions; indeed, to do this would be to wipe the notion of intertextuality off the map of literary theoretical analysis.

For some scholars the notion of intertextuality clearly plays an important role in people's understanding of the phenomenon of literature: both in its general form (literary and linguistic semantics) and in its modified versions useful in other, less general parts of literary theoretical investigation. Here, I want to draw attention to one particular suggestion derived from a modified version of intertextuality, which, in my opinion, indicates some of its important features and also provides for its further literary theoretical investigation. The theory of fictional worlds has, from the time it was first articulated in the 1980s, enriched literary theoretical investigation with several notions and strategies proven useful in the analysis of specific aspects of literary communication. Among other things, fictional-world theory offers, through one of its most important contributors, Lubomír Doležel and his *Heterocosmica*, the concept of *literary transduction*, which actually represents a certain alternative to the notion of intertextuality and seems to stand somewhat outside the mainstream approaches in this field. Nevertheless, the aim of my study is to investigate the term transduction critically and to analyse the possible potential this concept may have for intertextually related literary artworks.

For the genetic view of intertextuality, we can differentiate between particular levels and degrees of intertextual connections. At the most abstract level, all literary artworks are intertextually connected as such – belonging as they do to a literature and its traditions. Nevertheless, proper genetic connections between literary artworks can be distributed to particular sets according to their plots, characters, composition, prosaic/poetic form, metre, style, and so forth; consequently, we speak about particular genres and forms. As Jonathan Culler states: "A genre, one might say, is a conventional function of language, a particular relation to the world which serves as norm or expectation to guide the reader in his encounter with the text" (CULLER 1975: 136). Nevertheless, it must be stated that these norms or expectations are firmly connected with the author's intention, which is determined by their fictional encyclopedias. The encyclopedias anchor the literary communication within the artwork's period of literary development and govern the use of specific means employed to achieve certain effects on the readers.

When we claim that literary artworks are intertextually connected in terms of their genetic links, based in turn on their affiliation to certain genres and forms of the developing literary structure, we actually approach Bakhtin's aforementioned observation regarding words and their belonging to someone else. Nevertheless, as stated, this grasp of textuality brings scholars only to the very broadest and vaguest systems of intertextuality, which are thus of no great analytical value. Therefore, some theoreticians tend to think of intertextuality in a much narrower sense, which enables them to stipulate various sets of criteria and consequently use them for analyses of intertextual relationships between particular literary texts.

3. Transduction

In this subchapter, let us investigate one of the few conceptions that can be viewed as a variant of the type of intertextual investigation previously assigned as "particular" (see here pg. 73). This variant is connected with the term *transduction* and Lubomír Doležel's conception of fictional worlds.

3.1 Lubomír Doležel's view of intertextuality

Before we enter the investigation of the connection between transduction and fictional worlds semantics, it will be fruitful to focus in more detail on Doležel's conception of intertextuality. In his first step, Doležel moves the investigation of genetic relationships and textual types outside the realm of intertextuality. He assigns abstract genetic connections of texts *absolute intertextuality* and states that the "positioning of the novels within the web of intertextuality does not explain their character as individualized and identifiable literary works [...] The intratextual and intertextual ingredients interact in complex ways, but there is order in this chaos, the order of the emergent literary structure. Absolutized intertextuality does away not only with the originality but also with the historicity of literary texts, making them all just ripples in an anonymous intertextual flow" (DOLEŽEL 1998: 200). This conception of intertextuality can be useful only for a certain typology of literary artworks based on categories that are results of highly abstract procedures.

Doležel steps outside this circle and proposes "to view intertextuality not as an immutable law but as a historically changing factor of literary text production" (DOLEŽEL 1998: 200). Furthermore, he stands strictly against the temporary influences and genealogical connections in literary development: "It is becoming apparent that intertextual analysis differs from influence study in that it is focused on semantic interpretation" (201). Using this procedure Doležel actually makes two important moves: a) he abandons the pre-structuralist conception of investigation of cause and consequence, or of old and new, in the development of literary structure; and b) by connecting intertextuality with an interpretation of meaning he takes an important step toward incorporating his own conception of intertextuality into the framework of fictional world semantics.

In his next step, Doležel divides intertextuality into explicit and implicit kinds. The latter is more important for the study of intertextual relationships: "This kind of intertextuality is governed by the general conditions of implicitness [...] First, it is marked by *allusions*, which direct the interpreter from one literary text to other texts, to artworks, and so on. Second, it follows the basic rule of the semantic interpretation of implicitness: the text's meaning can be grasped without identifying the intertext but is enriched, often quite substantially, by its discovery" (DOLEŽEL 1998: 201). As we can see, Doležel's conception of an implicit texture and its uncovering represents the next stage in his general theory of the implicit meaning of literary texts. Here the textual intention has to meet the reader's encyclopedia and must intersect with the reader's ability to infer this kind of meaning. Intertextuality in this conception is thus viewed and treated as "a property of texture" (201). Nevertheless, continuing this way would lead the theoretician to the conception of intertextuality developed on mere textual similarities and therefore to the same vicious circle. This is why Doležel strictly stipulates that: "literary works are linked not only on the level of texture but also, and no less importantly, on the level of fictional worlds" (202). The texture is an important but not necessary precondition of the re-construction of a fictional world. It is fictional worlds as semiotic objects that exist outside their texts and come into important relationships.

3.2 Transduction and fictional worlds

A detailed examination of prototexts lies in the background of the inquiry of transduction: prototexts serve as the bases for a fictional world's creation. It is tempting to exchange the couple prototext vs. metatext for the couple proto-world vs. meta-world; however, this unconditional analogy would face several difficulties.

First of all, metatexts that are developed as a contribution of narrative prototexts are divided into two subsets: metatexts which are of a narrative essence and those which are not. The latter subset consists of theoretical and critical metatexts of a descriptive nature. These texts describe the original prototexts and their fictional world but do not themselves create fictional worlds. Such texts are of little use from the point of view of a world metamorphosis based on prototexts and metatexts. The second subset of metatexts is represented by a wider set of texts that have the ability to accommodate narrative fictional worlds. When classifying the ways in which particular texts are linked, we always have to keep in mind the two axes defined at the beginning of our intertextual thoughts (transparency/hiddeness and partiality/wholeness of succession). Nevertheless, for a more detailed investigation of the phenomenon under inquiry one should also consider the axis of intentionality/unintentionality on the part of the author. In the text in which the originator has placed some reference to other texts, the readers' competence is crucial for uncovering and interpreting this reference: the reader must be able to encode the text, must be able to comprehend it and also must possess a fictional encyclopedia, which enables him/her to connect one fictional world to another. Both these competences are essential for the reader to gain the semantic power to uncover and interpret potential intertextual relationships between particular texts and their worlds. Otherwise these relationships stay unread, covered, and thus do not play any role in the reader's re-creation of a fictional world (metaworld) with the contribution of a fictional proto-world.

3.3 Transduction as an alternative to intertextuality

At this point, it also becomes necessary to raise the following question for the realm of fictional worlds: Do not fictional worlds constitute a similarly complex network, as equally complicated for a detailed analytical investigation of intertextual connections as the traditional approaches? The simple answer to this question then would be: Yes, they do. However, at the same time, it must be added that fictional worlds display features that link literary artworks to various levels of literary meaning and therefore enable a possible comparison based on the analysis of these levels. This claim is not meant to imply that fictional worlds represent a completely innovative impulse to intertextual literary investigation: the inquiry of the relationships of fictional worlds stems from both the tradition of influences (as the investigation of the mutual relationships between literary texts has been called), and the tradition of intertextuality – in these respects it reflects both the genealogical and the stylistic features of fictional texts.

Doležel, when introducing his own view of intertextual relationships between fictional texts, takes as his starting point Riffaterre's differentiation between two sources of intertextual relationships: between particular texts and universal cultural stock ("sociolect") (cf. DOLEŽEL 1998: 200). This division prompts Doležel to suggest that an intertextual analysis "is focused on semantic interpretation," due to the fact that "through intertextuality, texts are bound together in a relationship of mutual semantic illumination" (201). Restricting intertextuality to the area of semantics enables Doležel not only to narrow the term to a form accessible by analytical means, but also to connect it with those semantic devices that constitute the very core of fictional worlds theory: "In terms of our semantics, this intertextuality is a constituent of the text's intensional meaning" (201). At this point, we can explain the significance of "intensional meaning" for fictional worlds. Doležel, using Gottlob Frege's distinction between *Bedeutung* (reference) and *Sinn* (sense), differentiates between extensional and intensional structures of fictional worlds: whereas the extension of an expression refers to a set of objects referred to by the expression, the intension is the way in which these objects are presented through particular expressions. In terms of fictional worlds, this division applies thus: whereas an extensional structure of a fictional world represents a set of objects referred to by a fictional text, an intensional structure of the world reflects the way in which this reference is constituted in an expression. In other words, extensional structures are the *Whats* referred to by fictional texts, while intensional structures are the *Hows* by which they are referred to. In the light of this division, the connection of the notion of intertextuality with the intensional aspects of fictional worlds is not surprising. Even less surprising is the way in which Doležel evaluates this kind of intertextuality for literary fictional inquiry: "But for a literary semantics that reinstates reference in general and fictional reference in particular, the purely intensional conception of intertextuality, despite its appeal and relevance, is insufficient" (201–202).

Consequently, instead of using the notion of intertextuality (which, in his view, does not offer a satisfactory theoretical background for an analytical investigation of the connections between fictional texts at every level), Doležel introduces the term *transduction*. The term was originally developed in the natural sciences and has been used in several areas of scientific investigation; such as, genetics, biophysics, and physiology, in order to describe a specific kind of material transfer between objects and structures, which retains some important, usually structured forms of the information transferred.

Fictional worlds have two important qualities which bring them in to close connection with the term transduction: i) they are, by definition, complexly structured entities carrying complex literary meaning at all those levels we traditionally connect with literary (narrative) meaning, the levels of which are (to a greater or lesser extent) analysable; ii) they are, again by definition, means of specific literary communication and as such are transferable. Nevertheless, the link between fictional worlds and intertextuality lies primarily in the fact that fictional worlds represent uniquely text-based entities.

The theory of fictional worlds, unlike theories which do not borrow from Frege's division between the extensional and intensional meaning of a linguistic expression, must investigate intertextual relationships at both levels of the structure of fictional worlds: "literary works are linked on both the intensional and the extensional level" (DOLEŽEL 1998: 202). It is exactly at this point that Doležel introduces the term transduction in order to describe these links: "I use the term *literary transduction* to encompass both kinds of lineage. Literary transduction thus supersedes and absorbs intertextuality" (202). Having been inspired by the general schema of (literary) communication, Doležel derives its modified version in order to describe the schema for literary transduction:

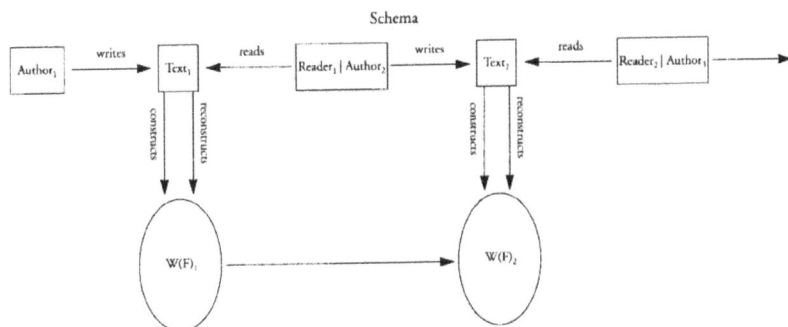

Schema

$$
\text{Author}_1 \xrightarrow{writes} \text{Text}_1 \xleftarrow{reads} \text{Reader}_1 \mid \text{Author}_2 \xrightarrow{writes} \text{Text}_2 \xleftarrow{reads} \text{Reader}_2 \mid \text{Author}_3 \longrightarrow
$$

$$
\text{Text}_1 \; \big\downarrow_{\text{constructs}} \; \big\uparrow^{\text{reconstructs}} \qquad \text{Text}_2 \; \big\downarrow_{\text{constructs}} \; \big\uparrow^{\text{reconstructs}}
$$

$$
W(F)_1 \longrightarrow W(F)_2
$$

As we can see, the schema expresses several essential preconditions: apart from the communicative fictional-worlds-based approach, it primarily offers the idea of a deliberate role for the $\text{Reader}_1/\text{Author}_2$ whose creative act of reading Text_1 results in a creative act of writing Text_2; thus, Doležel's idea of transductional intertextual relationships between literary texts is based on a deliberate *poiesis* that reflects its determination from the original fictional texts and results in a new text. This strict precondition actually enables Doležel to narrow down the number of all possible connections between particular fictional worlds and thus to avoid the problems faced by the notion of intertextuality in the sense of a network connecting all textual works. The second important precondition in Doležel's schema is his emphasis on the controlling power of the process of literary transduction: "The author is responsible for text production and world construction; his text functions as a kind of score in which the fictional world is inscribed. The reader's text processing and world reconstruction follow the instructions of the score" (205). This statement is to be read not only as the theoretician's objection to reader-focused approaches in literary theoretical inquiry, but also as a statement of the dependence of $Text_1$ ($World_1$) on $Text_2$ ($World_2$) and thus stipulates the precise direction of the process of literary transduction. Once the ranks and directions are claimed within this approach, one cannot fall into the trap of unlimited and nondirectional *poiesis* on the part of creation; on the other hand, on the part of reception, stipulating similar restrictions would be of no theoretical and aesthetic advantage. From the point of view of the reader's reception of fictional texts and creation of fictional worlds, it is not important which world is the substratic one and which is the superstratic one. It is not difficult to see that the fictional worlds developed by transductional processes constitute what can be viewed as chains. Their particular links can be considered specific semiotic units as such, but also as essential contributors to the meaning of the whole when perceived within the milieu of other links constituting the chain.

As already noted, fictional worlds structures consist of their extensional and intensional parts. In order to keep the two-pronged (extensional and intensional) structure of fictional worlds, not only for the original worlds but also for those subsequently developed by transductional procedures, it is necessary to define the relationships between extensional and intensional structures of both the original worlds and those developed in transduction. The first thing to say here is that these two structures in fictional worlds are indivisible: "Although extensions and intensions can and must be differentiated in semantic theory, they are by definition complementary in the production of literary meaning. Extensions are available only through intensions and, conversely, intensions are fixed by extensions. We can speculate that the author conceives the fictional world first as an extensional structure, inventing the story, individuating the acting persons in their properties and relationships, setting them in landscapes and cityscapes; then, by writing a text of a particular texture, they give an intensional shape to the world. Conversely, readers are presented first with the intensional structuring, since they access the fictional world through the text's texture; by information or formalized paraphrasing they translate the texture[39] into extensional representations and thus reconstruct the extensional world structure and its parts – story, character portraits, landscapes, and cityscapes" (DOLEŽEL 1998: 142–43).

As we have seen, intensional and extensional structures of fictional worlds are defined as inseparable and firmly connected in fictional meaning production. However, for the purpose of the investigation of fictional worlds, it can be

---

39 "Texture is the exact form of expression." (DOLEŽEL 1998:35)

fruitful to approach them discretely. Investigating them discretely enables us to use theoretical approaches developed in the realm of poetics, narrative theory, and theory of action for describing extensional structures, and the approaches developed in stylistics and literary semantics for describing intensional structures. Separating the two sets of means enables theoreticians, when investigating both types of fictional world structuration, to analyse fictional worlds as two-pronged entities. This division has proven itself an important tool by connecting fictional worlds semantics to already existing concepts; thus, this system both uses the already developed concepts and strategies and helps to specify and redefine them.

To be more specific, Doležel, when exemplifying the notion of literary transduction, actually specifies two types of (intertextual) connection between fictional works, which are encapsulated under the same notion. *Translation* and *postmodernist rewrite* represent, according to the author, the two most significant examples of literary transductional connection. In terms of translation, Doležel states: "The translator cannot render precisely the intensional meaning of the original texture, because the form of expression in the target language differs from that of the original language. But he or she is able, indeed, has the duty, to preserve the fictional world in its extensional structuring and, as far as possible, in its intensional structuring as well" (DOLEŽEL 1998: 205). In other words, the extensional structures of the fictional worlds of both the original text and that based on the translated text must be identical. As stated above, every extensional meaning is based in the exact texture of a literary work. Therefore, the textures of the original work and that of the work translated must create bases which have the potential to allow readers to create identical fictional words during the act of reading (or at least worlds which are as identical as possible). In this case the translator must not only fully preserve and transfer the extensional structure of the original world, but they also should subordinate the intensional structure of the set of stylistic and functional conventions in the target language. In other words, the intensional structures of the original and translated fictional worlds should be as identical as possible, regardless of the particular linguistic means and conventions underlying them. Here we can observe a strong functional claim that is, on the one hand, connected with functional linguistics and stylistics (as suggested by the Prague School), and with functional translatology (as proclaimed in the work of Jiří Levý) on the other.[40]

Nevertheless, translation is not the only transductional procedure Doležel identifies and analyses. The second major set of texts created by transduction is

---

40 As it is formulated especially in his *Umění překladu*, 1963 (*The Art of Translation*).

represented by a rewritten text founding specific fictional worlds that are in close connection with the fictional worlds of the original texts and thus fulfil a specific aesthetic function. Doležel, from among the whole set of rewrites, chooses one specific type and draws his theoretical attention to the postmodernist rewrite. In the case of the postmodern rewrite the connection between the original and the rewritten worlds (both functioning as the means of specific aesthetic communication) can be described quite specifically: "the rewrite not only confronts the canonical fictional world with contemporary aesthetic and ideological postulates but also provides the reader with a familiar space within the strange landscapes of radical postmodernist experimentation" (DOLEŽEL 1998: 206). In order to move beyond this very general level, Doležel consequently offers a typology of the most typical worlds constructed by postmodern rewriting: they are either *parallel, complementary* or *polemical* to the original worlds. Whereas the first type of worlds adapt the original story to different temporal-spatial placements, the second type fills in the gaps of the original world, and finally, the third type is based on the negation of the original protoworld. Nevertheless, all the types of worlds mentioned here, created by the processes of postmodernist rewriting, share one essential quality: "All postmodernist rewriters *re*design, *re*locate, *re*valuate the classic protoworld" (206). From all that has been said so far, it should be clear that postmodernist rewrites create worlds that can be very close to their protoworlds, but that are also very detached from and actually contradictory to them. If so, an important question must arise: is there a "sufficiency condition" for protoworlds and their rewrites that allows us to say that the rewritten world is connected to the original world, to the extent that we can claim that the rewrite is the result of a transductional procedure applied to the protoworld? Doležel suggests that these connections can be found at several fictional world levels: "We start by aligning the protowork and its presumed rewrite on the basis of some strong textural and structural evidence – the title, the quotations, the intertextual allusions, the similarity of the fictional worlds structure, the homology of agential constellations, the parallelism of the story lines, the like setting. Only when we have strong enough evidence for the rewrite hypothesis will we draw the transworld identity lines. Some of these lines will link individuals with different names" (226). Only when similar individuals can be identified across different fictional worlds, together with other structural similarities of these worlds (landscapes and social structures), can we identify the worlds as connected by the procedure of transduction. Unlike translated worlds, which are predetermined by the intensional structures of the original worlds, in the case of rewritten worlds it is primarily the extensional structure that matters.

To sum up, we can say that the notion of transduction as introduced above actually does represent a variant of intertextual inquiry. Using the concept of fictional worlds, the theory claims that the connection between literary artworks can be described only at the level of the worlds – complex structured entities that carry literary meaning at several levels. Thus, in order to stipulate a firm connection between protoworlds and derived worlds, the theory stipulates that the connection be present at several world-levels. The notion of transduction is thus used for the description of a relatively small set of interconnected literary texts – in exact opposition to the vaguely defined networks of intertextual links present in some conceptions mentioned at the start of this chapter. This conclusion supports the idea that the set of literary artworks connected by intertextual links stands in reciprocal proportion to the set of criteria applied to the artworks for the purpose of analysing their intertextual connections. As much as the notion of transduction encompasses a relatively wide set of necessary connections between fictional worlds in order to claim those worlds (intertextually) connected by transduction, the set of works themselves linked by transduction is limited to translations and postmodern rewrites. By contrast, the more general the preconditions of intertextuality, the wider the set of literary texts to which they apply. Thus, while transduction does not represent phenomena salient with regard to intertextuality, it can nevertheless helpful analyse connections between artworks that are individually conceived and developed.

IV. The Prague School and fictional worlds

In this part of my study, I focus on three related stages in fictional worlds research: in the first part I show the way in which the modern state of fictional worlds semantics is grounded in the linguistic investigations of the Prague School; in the second I elaborate on the way that Prague School linguistics contributed to the final design of one specific system of fictional world semantics, that of Lubomír Doležel; and finally in the third part I examine a new and highly interesting version of fictional worlds which connects Doležel's work with the heritage of the Prague School – a study of the fictional worlds of lyric poetry by Miroslav Červenka.

1. Linguistics and aesthetics

When using the term *Prague School,* we usually refer to both branches of Czech structuralist inquiry: linguistics and aesthetics. Thus, on the one hand, we delineate two different fields of investigation, but on the other hand we acknowledge two methodologically similar (unified) approaches which result in a specifically shaped literary-theoretical inquiry: both disciplines share the same interest in one of the most important types of works of art, that of the literary artwork. Whereas practitioners of the former focus more on the material of their artworks, the latter takes into account their milieu and development; but both disciplines are primarily concerned with the artwork's function. Thus, at the intersection of structuralist linguistics and aesthetics Prague School, literary theory is born.

In the global context, Prague School linguistics primarily refers to its functional aspect. In fact, we commonly speak about Prague School functional linguistics in particular. I do not want to suggest that it was Prague School scholars who brought the term *function* to the field of linguistic investigation; nevertheless, it seems that it was Prague School scholars who started using this term in a specific and rather influential way, both in their system of linguistic inquiry and in their analyses of particular linguistic units. The concept of functional linguistics is based on the assumption, borrowed from the general model of communication, that particular language statements do not hang in the air on their own but are specific messages from a sender to a receiver in the act of language communication. These messages are designed in order to carry specific meaning, regardless of whether we are describing everyday non-literary communication or communication through literary artworks: "The sender in the act of speaking follows some aims/functions and according to the aims uses specific language devices, a specific functional language" (STARÝ 1995: 36). This assumption inevitably triggered the Prague School scholars' interest in the general problem of language use and effect. The communicational aspect of language units is thus thoroughly intertwined with the pragmatic view of language and its structures.[41]

Generally speaking, the aforementioned communicative basis of the Prague School theory of functional styles plays a crucial role not only in Prague School linguistics but also in its aesthetics. As we shall see, this aspect determines the very idea of aesthetic communication between author and reader and also grounds the notion of the *aesthetic function* – one of the key aspects of the Prague School aesthetic system. Nevertheless, on the level of linguistics (or stylistics) the functional model brings Prague School scholars to two major fields of linguistic investigation which are of great importance for literary-theoretical inquiry: to the analysis of narrative models and situations (an important part of general narratological scholarship to the present day) and to the study of poetic language, which provokes the issue of the identity of literary artworks. Indeed, the focus on the internal structures of linguistic statements and the effect these statements may have on the receiver represents the core of Prague School structuralist aesthetics, based on the concept of aesthetic function. Aesthetic function, according to Jan Mukařovský's definition, focuses the reader's attention on the structure of a literary artwork on the way in which the artwork is composed and on the language in which the artwork is written.

2. Literary theory

Using the idea of functional styles to attempt a definition of the identity of the literary, Prague structuralists tried to show and investigate further the difference between common (practical) and poetic languages. At this point we encounter one of the most important resemblances between the Prague School and the Russian formalists, who attempted to define literature by the use of poetic language, the material of literary artworks.[42] However, from a contemporary point

---

41 Today it is well known that the pragmatic inquiry results into one of the crucial achievements of Prague School research which has been evaluated and pointed out by the scholars of the so called Constance School.

42 It is obvious that the very idea of poetic language does not originate within the framework of Russian formalist thought. Nevertheless, in this framework the search for poetic language results in the crucial question of the identity of literary artworks which in turn results in the idea of the poetic function. The idea of the poetic function of

of view it is obvious that to differentiate between poetic and common languages is to walk on very thin ice. As Roman Jakobson observed: "But even if we succeed in isolating those devices that typify the poets of a given period, we have still to establish the line of demarcation between poetry and nonpoetry. The same alliterations and other types of euphonic devices are used by the rhetoric of the period; and what is more they occur in everyday, colloquial language. Streetcar conversations are full of jokes based on the very figures found in the most subtle lyric poetry, and the composition of gossip often corresponds to the laws of composition followed by best sellers, or at least last year's best sellers (depending on the degree of the gossiper's intelligence)" (JAKOBSON 1981: 741). One way of negotiating this problem suggested by Prague School scholars is the following: from the whole list of potential functions that are intended to be fulfilled and can actually be fulfilled in the act of linguistic communication, they chose *the aesthetic function* and stipulated its *dominance* in specific literary communication.

According to Mukařovský, the aesthetic function substantially determines the identity of literary artworks and literary aesthetic communication as a whole. The aesthetic function is initiated by the subject (receiver) of a communication and transmitted by the literary artwork, the object of the communication: "But an active capacity for the aesthetic function is not a real property of an object, even if the object has been deliberately composed with the aesthetic function in mind. Rather, the aesthetic function manifests itself only under certain conditions, i. e., in a certain social context. A phenomenon which, in one time period, country, etc., was the privileged bearer of the aesthetic function may be incapable of bearing this function in a different time, country, etc." (MUKAŘOVSKÝ 1970: 3). However, in spite of the fact that the aesthetic function is initially triggered by the subject of an aesthetic communication, the literary work itself is shaped (structured) according to the purpose of the communication and therefore its structure enables the subject to trigger the aesthetic function. In other words, the literary artwork, having been specifically designed for aesthetic communication, enables the perceiving subject (the reader) to take the *aesthetic stance*, which is the essential precondition of aesthetic functioning. Nevertheless, with regard to the idea of poetic language two simple questions remain: What is the connection between poetic language and aesthetic function? And how is the function based in language?

To answer these questions, we must bear in mind another crucial point of Prague structuralism. According to Prague aesthetics an artwork is of a *sign*

Russian formalists brings them to the notion of an artistic method (prijom) which substantially contributed to the modern narratological environment.

nature; therefore, the artwork refers to reality in order not to reach any other aim than aesthetic pleasure. In other words, a literary artwork, which is essentially a sign, has a specific reference. It does not primarily refer to *What is said* but also, and more strongly, to *How it is said* – the way a poetic language distorts our everyday common sense catches the reader's attention and aims it at the structure of the work itself. At this point, we can come to the conclusion that we are bound in a circle: poetic language determines aesthetic function, which in turn helps the reader to employ an aesthetic stance and thus to trigger the aesthetic function – and the function focuses the reader's attention back onto the poetic language. Fortunately, the framework of the Prague School aesthetics offers us more to work with: it defines procedures which operate in poetic language and its development – that of *actualisation* and *automatisation*.[43] It must be emphasised, however, that they both do so at all levels of the linguistic structure of an artwork and thus can be viewed only as a part of the overall structure of literary development, in a process of change.[44] But what are the concrete manifestations of a language of this kind? According to Czech structuralists, in every literary artwork we find both poetic devices and strategies which we consider traditional (or well-known), as well as devices and strategies which are newly used; however, the combination of these affects the reader's reception and focuses their attention on the specific combination of the devices.

At this point, we can see one of the most important anticipations of fictional worlds semantics: research into narrative modes. When trying to analyse and describe the procedures of automatisation and actualisation in the development of poetic language, some structuralists, notably Mukařovský and Felix Vodička,

---

43 The Prague School shares the idea of automatisation and actualisation with Russian formalism; however, whereas Russian formalists refer to this idea mainly in order to differentiate poetic language from common language, in Czech structuralism the idea represents an important aspect of the analysis of literary development. Let us emphasise that in the framework of Prague linguistics we can find a strong emphasis placed on the dynamic characteristics of language development. Not surprisingly, the developmental aspect of literary structures had been established in Prague literary criticism in a more complicated and more gradual fashion.

44 The concept of literary development in connection with the identity of literature within the Prague School inquiry is based on two major theoretical sources. First of all, Russian formalists, when defying the identity of literature in the final stage of Formal School, came to the idea of literary development; this idea is directly derived from the formalist search for poetic language. The second source of Prague School concept of literary development is based on the Hegelian idea of history and development; from this idea the Prague School theoreticians derived their idea of immanent literary development.

were seriously involved in the detailed analyses of various levels and forms of narration and narratives. Not surprisingly, one of their levels of interest was closely connected with the further narratological investigation of so called narrative modes or narrative situations. In their studies from the 1920s to 1940s Mukařovský and Vodička, in order to describe larger elements of narratives and their historical developments, tried to analyse the narratives' inner linguistic structures in connection with such terms as plot, the narrator, literary character, subject and object of narration, monologue and dialogue, first-person narration and third-person narration, objectivity and subjectivity of narration, truth-values, or perspective in narration. Since that time, this specific approach to the analysis of narratives and narrativity has been part and parcel of the Czech structuralist approach to literature, namely narration. Historically speaking, Doležel is a direct ancestor of this tradition and has not only provided modern literary theory with a systemic analysis of narrative *modes*, but also with a crucial contribution to *fictional worlds semantics*.

With respect to the theory of fictional worlds, it must be emphasised that apart from the emphasis placed on stylistic analyses of aesthetic texts the Prague School structuralists have employed another important notion in their investigation of narratives that is essentially involved in the contemporary form of these worlds: the notion of a literary or fictitious world itself. Of course, the notion of a world created by an artwork can barely be considered new in the first half of the twentieth century, when the core of this structuralist field of investigation develops;[45] however, within the Prague School inquiry a literary-artwork-created world is a highly structured entity which is dependent on the structure of the work as a whole, and thus necessarily bound to other narrative levels and entities. Whereas in the work of Mukařovský we seldom find suggestions referring to entities that can be viewed as structured literary worlds,[46] the system provided by

---

45 It seems that the first scholar to be involved in the investigation of literary worlds in Czech lands was Josef Jungman in his canonical book *Slowesnost* in 1825. Nevertheless, the concept of literary worlds comes to the Czech lands from abroad and is considerably older – see in particular Lubomír Doležel's *Occidental Poetics* (1989), which provides the reader with a detailed historical overview of particular conceptions of literary worlds.

46 Jan Mukařovský infrequently refers to certain narrative contexts which can be viewed as entities similar to worlds of fiction; in his study of Božena Němcová, Mukařovský refers to "plot enviroment"; in the study of Karel Čapek's epics he uses the term "reality we speak about." The history of usage of the notion *world* in the history of Czech literary studies is thoroughly described by Ondřej Sládek, who ultimately states that the

Vodička explicitly employs the term *outer world*: "Under the term *outer world* we do not understand only a material environment but also the whole social, mental and ideological atmosphere in which literary characters and also plots take place [...] Both the plot as well as characters are involved in a world alongside their space and time aspects; therefore, in a literary artwork motifs exist that refer to the outer world. These motifs in fact create a specific continuous context, which serves as a base for fictional characters during the whole story" (VODIČKA 1948: 114). What has to be emphasised at this point is that whereas previously, worlds of art were maintained as images that are derived, in various ways, and to different extents, from the world of our reality, Vodička's outer worlds are entities that assume an important position in his system of narratological inquiry. They are a part of the basis for the stories in which outer worlds can be viewed in specific constellations together with other elements, which according to Vodička follow a specific logic imposed by the narration itself. This part of Prague School narratological investigation seems to be partially present in the way that the contemporary semantics of fictional worlds maintains these worlds as specifically designed and shaped semiotic entities, ones which can occupy various positions in their relations to the real (actual) world (or to other worlds). Nevertheless, even in Vodička's system, outer worlds can be viewed as narratological entities but not yet as semiotic ones – this privilege is reserved only for fictional worlds.

3. Fictional worlds

We can summarise by saying that both the investigation of narrative modes as well as the notion of a specific literary world, which is important for the further development of fictional worlds semantics, are present in Doležel's systemic approach to fictional worlds. They are, in turn, involved in his idea of intensional and extensional structures of fictional worlds. In sum, the extensional structure of a fictional world refers to *What entities and events are narrated (What is narrated)*, whereas the intensional structure refers to *How it is narrated*. Whereas extensional structures of narrative texts refer to fictional world's paraphrasable structures of "What is happening in the worlds," intensional structures of fictional narrative texts refer to "How it is said," to the form of the text expression itself.

---

relationship between fictional worlds and the previous theoretical concepts containing worlds is "neither direct nor uncomplicated" (SLÁDEK 2015: 144).

Thus, Doležel's approach connects an extensive study of the formal features of narrative modes with a functional point of view: narrative modes are speech acts with specific functions within narrative structures. In this part of his system Doležel combines the achievements of modern speech and action theory with the specific heritage of Prague School linguistics – that of its functional stylistics.

At the end of this section it is necessary to suggest that, whereas the extensional part of Doležel's theory is inspired by modern narratological investigation on the one hand and by theory of action on the other, the source of inspiration of its intensional part can be traced back to the core of Prague School linguistics and literary theory. I do not wish to claim that Doležel adopted all of the Prague School's crucial suggestions (for example, he leaves aside the essential notion of the aesthetic function). Nevertheless, the intensional part of his fictional world is strongly connected with the Prague School's method of stylistic inquiry.

Let us emphasise that among other concepts considered crucial to the Czech literary theoretical environment unaddressed by Doležel there is the notion of the *subject* in literature. Therefore, in this last section, I would like to draw attention to the way in which Miroslav Červenka, another prominent scholar of the Prague School, contributed to the fictional worlds semantics. This contribution is of special importance for two reasons: first, Červenka belonged to that group of direct descendents of the Prague School in the fields of aesthetics and versology, and secondly, he consequently tried to apply fictional world semantics to these two traditional fields of Czech structuralist investigation.

The aim of this chapter was to present some aspects of fictional worlds in the wider perspective of Czech structuralist tradition. What I would like emphasise at the very end is that the way in which fictional worlds are based (to an extent) in aspects of Prague structuralist thought enables us not only to confront them with the structuralist tradition itself, but also to apply them back to a tradition of scholarship and thus enrich that tradition with different perspectives and stimuli.

In his book, *Fictional Worlds of Lyric Poetry* (2003), Červenka significantly redesigns standard fictional worlds semantics with regard to the crucial topics of traditional Prague School investigation. Let us start with the statement that a fictional world represents the ultimate framework for a work's meaning—which lies at the very core of fictional world semantics—does not seem to be shared by all theoreticians involved in the analysis of fictional worlds. Some of them suggest that the meaning constructed by a literary artwork cannot be reduced to a fictional world and that fictional worlds are only parts of a meaningful game between the writer and the reader: to these game-worlds, metaphorically speaking, "the originator of the work, its implied subject, invites the perceiver"[47] (ČERVENKA 2005: 750). The subject, or hypothetical originator, of an artwork is, according to this approach, superior to a fictional world, which is just an object of their game: "The fictional world of a lyric poem is represented by its subjects" (ČERVENKA 2005: 728). Coming from the Prague School's investigation of the role of the subject in the process of literary communication, Červenka expresses his reservations towards the ultimate meaningfulness of fictional worlds, using lyric poetry as a counter-example: "It seems that that for demarcation of the work's subject it is necessary to argue with contemporary narratology and also to a lesser extent with fictional world semantics. Even Doležel, who approaches the meaningful activity of literary elements in a very sensitive way, [...] comes from an assumption that a fictional world is identical with the meaningful wholeness constituted by an artwork [...] Nevertheless, regarding lyric poetry, [...] the semantics of the work refers to the subject who created the work and therefore cannot be a part of its fictional world" (749–750).

Červenka uses Walton's suggestion in order to formulate the accessibility relation between a fictional world and the actual one: "A fictional world consists of certain levels, and so does the actual world. Each of them pushes out some of its domain towards the other and the worlds are mutually accessible thanks to these border transitional regions. On the side of the actual world this domain is a demarcated domain of game; on the side of the fictional world this domain is embodied in the subject and determined by the way in which the fictional is treated during the game. In the world of game, not only do the real speaker and receiver meet, but also their fictional counterparts" (ČERVENKA 2005: 716). As we can see, Červenka's reservations towards Doležel's conception come from the poetological tradition of the Prague School, which understands a literary artwork as a specific aesthetic object whose constructed meaning refers to the work's subject. Consequently, Červenka rejects the reduction of the aesthetic object to a fictional world and refuses to submit the work's subject (which is, according to his conception, the ultimate work's meaning base) to the fictional work: "Here especially, in this uncertain domain—not of a fictional world of the work, but of the way in which this world is treated— the work's subject is placed as a hypothetical carrier of creative acts that have led to the origin of the work" (750). Červenka understands the notion of fictional worlds in a sense employed by Mukařovský and

---

47   Here, Červenka borrows the term *world of game* from Kendall Walton – see WALTON 1990.

Vodička; however, he pays substantially greater attention to this concept than his two prominent forebears of the Prague School.

At the same time, Červenka also refuses to understand fictional worlds as the result of a joint creative power of intensional functions. Intensional functions in Červenka's conception refer outside a fictional world, to the world of game of which the fictional world is an object. In Doležel conception it would be possible to suggest that a fictional world merges with the work's subject – if only the term "subject" was one used in his theory. It is very difficult to compare Doležel's single-level conception (fictional world) with the two-level conception of Červenka, quality for quality. Whereas the former derives from the tradition of general literary semiotics, the latter builds on the aesthetic heritage of the Prague School. Therefore, they both coexist as two possible alternatives of one (worldly) approach.

Literature

ALLÉN, Sture (ed.) 1989: *Possible Worlds in Humanities, Arts and Sciences.* Walter de Gruyter, Berlin and New York.

ALLWOOD, J. & ANDERSSON, L.-G. & DAHL, Ö. 1977: *Logic in Linguistics.* Cambridge University Press: Cambridge.

AUSTIN, J. L. 1971: *How to Do Things with Words.* Oxford University Press: London.

BAKHTIN, Michail 1984: *Problems of Dostoevsky's Poetics.* University of Minnesota Press, Minneapolis. (Trans. Caryl Emerson)

BRADLEY, R. & SCHWARTZ, N.1979: *Possible Worlds: An Introduction to Logic and its Philosophy.* Hackett Publishing Company, Indianapolis.

CARNAP, Rudolf 1955: Meaning and synonymy in natural languages. *Philosophical Studies*, vol. 6, no. 3, pgs. 33–47.

CULLER, Jonathan 1975: *Structuralist Poetics. Structuralism, Linguistics and the Study of Literature.* Cornell University Press, Ithaca.

ČERVENKA, Miroslav 2005: Fikční světy lyriky. In Hodrová, D., Hrbata, Z., Vojtková, M. (eds). *Na cestě ke smyslu: Poetika literárního díla 20. Století.* Torst, Praha, pgs. 711–783.

HUGHES, G. & E. CRESSWELL, M. J. 1968: *An Introduction to Modal Logic.* Methuen and Co., London.

CRESSWELL, M. J. 1985: *Structured Meanings. The Semantics of Propositional Attitudes.* The MIT Press, Cambridge. 1988 *Semanticall Essays: Possible Worlds and Their Rivals.* Kluwer Academic Publishers, Dordrecht.– Boston.– London.

van DIJK, Teun A.: 1973 Models for Text Grammars. In Bogdan, Radu J. ? Niinilkoto, Ilkka (eds.): *Logic, Language, and Probability.* D. Reidel Publishing Company, Boston.

DOLEŽEL, Lubomír 1989: *Occidental Poetics. Tradition and Progress.* University of Nebraska Press, Lincoln and London. 1998 *Heterocosmica. Fiction and Possible Worlds.* The John Hopkins University Press, Baltimore and London. 2010 *Possible Worlds of Fiction and History: The Postmodern Stage.* The John Hopkins University Press, Baltimore and London.

ECO, Umberto 1990: *The Limits of Interpretation.* Indiana University Press, Bloomington and Indianapolis.

GIRLE, Rod 2000:. *Modal Logic and Philosophy.* McGill-Queen's University Press, Montreal – Kingston.

HEYDRICH, Wolfgang 1989: Possible Worlds and Enkvist's World. In Allén, S. (ed.) *Possible Worlds in Humanities, Arts and Sciences*. Walter de Gruyter, Berlin and New York.

HINTIKKA, Jaakko 1983:. Situations, Possible Worlds, and Attitudes. *Synthese* 54, pgs. 153–162.

CHIHARA, Charles S.1998: *The Worlds of Possibility*. Oxford University Press, Oxford.

JAKOBSON, Roman 1981: What Is Poetry. In *Selected Writings/III*. Mouton Publishers, The Hague – Paris – New York.

KAFKA, Franz 2000: Metamorphosis and Other Stories. Transl. M. Pasley. Penguin Books, London.

KOTEN, Jiří 2011: Fictional Worlds and Storyworlds: Forms and Means of Classification. In Fořt, B., Jedličková, A., Koten, J., Sládek, O. *Four Studies of Narrative*. ÚČL AVČR, Praha, pgs. 47–58.

KRIPKE, Saul A.1980: *Naming and Necessity*. Harvard University Press, Cambridge.

KRISTEVA, Julia 1980: *Desire in Language: A Semiotic Approach to Literature and Art*. Columbia University Press, New York. (Trans. E. Gora)

KUTSCHERA, Franz 1975: *Philosophy of Language*. D. Riedel Publishing Co., Boston.

LINSKY, Leonard 1969: Reference, Essentialism, and Modality. The Journal of Philosophy, vol. 66, no. 20, pgs. 687–700.

LEVÝ, Jiří 1963: *Umění překladu*. Československý spisovatel, Praha. 1971 *Paralipomena*. Československý spisovatel, Praha.

LEWIS, David K. 1968: Counterpart Theory and Quantified Modal Logic. *The Journal of Philosophy*, vol. LXV, no. 5, 1968; pgs. 113–126. 1973 *Counterfactuals*. Harvard University Press, Cambridge.

MARTÍNEZ-BONATI, Félix 1981: *Fictive Discourse and the Structures of Literature*. Cornell University Press, Ithaca and London.

MATERNA, Pavel 1998: *Concepts and Objects*. Acta Philosophica Fennica, Helsinki.

McHALE, Brian 1987: *Postmodernist Fiction*. Methuen, New York and London.

MONTAGUE, Richard 1974: *Formal Philosophy. Selected Papers of Richard Montague*. Yale University Press, New Haven.

MUKAŘOVSKÝ, Jan 1970: *Aesthetic Function, Norm and Value as Social Facts*. Ann Arbor.

PARSONS, Terence 1999: *Nonexistent Objects*. Yale University Press, New Haven and London.

PARTEE, Barbara H. 1989: Possible Worlds in Model – Theoretic Semantics: A Linguistics Perspective. In Allén, S. (ed.) *Possible Worlds in Humanities, Arts and Sciences*. Walter de Gruyter, Berlin and New York.

PAVEL, Thomas G. 1986: *Fictional Worlds*. Harvard University Press, Cambridge and London.

PEREGRIN, Jaroslav 1996: Úvod: Pavel Tichý a jeho logika. In Tichý, P. *O čem mluvíme? Vybrané stati k logice a sémantice*. FILOSOFIA, Praha. 1998 *Úvod do teoretické sémantiky*. Karolinum, Praha.

PLANTINGA, Alvin 1974: *The Nature of Necessity*. Oxford University Press, London.

PRIOR, A. N. & FINE, Kit 1977: *Worlds, Times, and Selves*. Duckworth, London.

QUINE, Willard Van Orman 1967: *Elementary Logic*. Harvard University Press, Cambridge. 1981 *Theories and Things*. Harvard University Press, Cambridge.

RASTIER, François 2000: *Meaning and Textuality*. University of Toronto Press, Toronto.

RESCHER, Nicholas 1975: *A Theory of Possibility*. University of Pittsburgh Press, Piisburgh.

RIFFATERRE, Michael 1959: Criteria for Style Analysis. *Word* 15, pgs. 154–174.

RONEN, Ruth 1994: *Possible Worlds in Literary Theory*. Cambridge University Press, Cambridge 1994.

RYAN, Marie-Laure 1991: *Possible Worlds, Artificial Intelligence, and Narrative Theory*. Indiana University Press, Bloomington and Indianapolis.

SLÁDEK, Ondřej 2015: *The Metamorphoses of Prague School Structural Poetics*. Lincom, Muenchen.

STARÝ, Zdeněk 1995: *Ve jménu funkce a intervence*. Karolinum, Praha.

TICHÝ, Pavel 1975: What Do We Talk About? Philosophy of Science, vol. 42, no. 1, pgs. 80–93. 1988 *The Foundations of Frege's Logic*. De Gruyter, Berlin.–New York.

VODIČKA, Felix 1948: Počátky krásné prózy novočeské. Melantrich, Praha.

WALTON, Kendall L. 1990: *Mimesis as Make-Believe: On the Foundations of the Representional Arts*. Harvard University Press, Cambridge – London.

WOLTERSTORFF, Nicholas 1980: *Works and Worlds of Art*. Oxford University Press, Oxford.

Literary and Cultural Theory

General editor: Wojciech H. Kalaga

www.peterlang.com

.